PREDATORS LIVE *Among Us*

Protect Your Family From Child Sexual Abuse

Diane Roblin-Lee

Foreword by

Melodie Bissell

Library and Archives Canada Cataloguing in Publication

Roblin-Lee, Diane, 1945-
Predators live among us [electronic resource] : protect your family from child sexual abuse / Diane Roblin-Lee ; foreword by Melodie Bissell.

Includes bibliographical references.
Electronic monograph.
ISBN 978-1-927355-00-8

1. Child sexual abuse--Prevention. 2. Child sexual abuse. 3. Child molesters. I. Title.

HV6570.R643 2012 362.76'7 C2012-904167-X

Published by
Castle Quay Books
1307 Wharf Street, Pickering, Ontario, L1W 1A5
Tel: (416) 573-3249
E-mail: *info@castlequaybooks.com*
www.castlequaybooks.com

Cover and interior layout and design: Diane Roblin-Lee *www.bydesignmedia.ca*

Disclaimer: The opinions expressed in this booklet are those of the author and do not constitute part of the curriculum of any program. The development, preparation and publication of this work has been undertaken with great care. However, the author, publisher, editors, employees and agents of *Winning Kids Inc.*, are not responsible for any errors contained herein or for consequences that may ensue from use of materials or information contained in this work. The information contained herein is intended to assist communities, churches and individuals in establishing effective response to a controversial issue and is distributed with the understanding that it does not constitute legal or medical advice. References to quoted sources are only as current as the date of the publications and do not reflect subsequent changes in law. Organizations, communities and individuals are strongly encouraged to seek legal counsel as well as counsel from an insurance company when establishing any policy concerned with this topic.

Purpose

How could a wife be married for 38 years and not know her husband had begun to molest children 25 years prior to being charged? It sounds impossible, but that was my experience. Because it is obviously very difficult to recognize the predators who live among us, I have researched and written this book in an attempt to bring something positive out of the devastation exacted upon our family. By sharing my hard-won insight, I hope to help parents and grandparents be more effective in protecting their little ones and escape the shattering fallout of child sexual abuse.

The purpose behind *Predators Live Among Us – Protect Your Family From Child Sexual Abuse* is sevenfold:

- to deter people who are fantasizing about molesting a child from acting on their fantasies
- to protect children from molestation through raising awareness on many levels
- to look at the new challenges of parenting in the 21st Century
- to deepen the understanding of all levels of society affected by the molestation of a child
- to find healing for victims and families
- to encourage the kind of justice and community action that prevents predators from initial offending and re-offending
- to demonstrate to all those who have been molested that I, and many others who labour to protect children, care very deeply about what you have endured and, in honour of you, are doing all we can to protect other children from sharing your experience.

Diane Roblin-Lee

Contents

Foreword

I am so thankful for the day I met Diane Roblin-Lee. We met in an elegant tea house for afternoon tea and scones. We were surrounded by beauty and grace! However, the topic of conversation was one with which we both felt God had burdened our hearts. It was the darkest of topics – child maltreatment and sexual abuse. I had found a new friend who shared my ever increasing burden and passion for the protection of children and youth. Diane had just completed a project of research and writing on the topic. *Winning Kids Inc.*® had the audience to read it.

In *Plan to Protect*™, the *Winning Kids Inc.*® protection plan for children, youth and those that work with them, we (the authors of *Plan to Protect*™), have dedicated an entire module to the reporting and response of abuse.

I wish I could say that, with the focus and attention abuse prevention and protection protocol has received over the last decade, the incidences of child sexual abuse are decreasing. I wish I could say that people seldom need to refer to this module. However, the maltreatment of children is on the rise. The exploitation of children globally is one of society's most shameful preoccupations.

Children are at risk! They are at risk in our communities, churches, schools, play grounds and sporting arenas; children are at risk even in our own homes!

Having been profoundly impacted personally, Diane recognizes the risk. But have we as a society, community, church, family, not *all* been profoundly impacted? The children certainly have been.

Francis T. Murphy, Presiding Justice (retired) of the Appellate Division, Supreme Court said,

> "Children have neither power nor property. Voices other than their own must speak for them. If those voices are silent, then children who are victims of abuse may lean their heads against window panes and take the bitter emptiness of violated childhoods."

Thank you Diane for speaking on behalf of the children!

Every parent and care-giver, and everyone working with children and youth should read *Predators Live Among Us: Protect Your Family From Child Sexual Abuse*. On behalf of the children, I ask you to please take the contents seriously. If you aren't convinced that we need to step up our efforts to protect them, I implore you to research this topic. The more I read, the more diligent and dedicated I am to winning the race against abuse.

Please join us!

On behalf of the children,

Melodie Bissell
President
Winning Kids Inc.® / Plan to Protect™

www.winningkidsinc.ca
Suite 14, A7-1390 Major Mackenzie Dr. E.
Richmond Hill, ON Canada L4S 0A1
1-877-455-3555

> *"But when they were oppressed they cried out to You. From heaven You heard them, and in Your great compassion You gave them deliverers, who rescued them from the hand of their enemies."* Nehemiah 9:27

1 one

Why all the Fuss?

Not too many years ago, there was something called "childhood"—a carefree time of life when Little League, hopscotch and pushing doll carriages down the sidewalk filled the rambling thoughts of children. As sun rays lengthened over the carefree days, parents would call sweaty youngsters in from play for baths and bedtime stories. "Johnnnnny...Susie...." The voices would trill through soft summer evenings, over backyard fences, down safe streets to the ears of children intent upon the games of the moment.

As the young ones grew, the games of the moment normally changed to include degrees of sexual experimentation. Kids found out 'how things happened' when they were ready—in their own time, ideally through healthy family discussions. The innocence of childhood gave way to adolescent discovery of the reproductive process and eventually—hopefully—to a satisfactory sex life in adulthood.

While that might now be scorned as the 'Beaver Cleaver' experience (suggesting unreality), the fact is that it was the general experience of the majority of North Americans upward into the 1960s. But now we live in a different world.

From Ward Cleaver to Homer Simpson

In the time it took for Ward Cleaver and the Fonze to morph into Homer Simpson and his South Park neighbors, the fiber of humanity changed. Once-safe sidewalks, filled with active children, emptied into avenues where anxious parents now drive their children to school. Parks became places to watch for strangers who lurk suspiciously around playgrounds. Hugs from teachers were replaced by lessons on "good-touch / bad-touch." The gentle priest became a questionable figure in the parish. Uncle Jack lost his time-honoured mantle of trustworthiness.

Like the frog sitting comfortably in a pan of warm water, not noticing the increase in temperature until it was too late, the world gradually lost its innocence. It seems incomprehensible to parents lulled to sleep by the innocuous Cleavers that they could suddenly wake up to the irreverent Simpsons, only to discover the deterioration wrought on society in the transition from Beaver to Bart.

Those who grew up watching "Happy Days" enjoyed the normal indulgence of adolescence where one delights in a certain arrogance that offends others. That mind-set unlocked the doors for those who sought to devalue the moral code of the day. It opened the floodgates for the reception of media programming and Internet content that demeaned integrity, decency and human character.

Now that we've grown up and regard that youthful arrogance as foolish immaturity, it's too late to push back the flood. But while Beaver Cleaver has become a societal aberration, society in general is still stuck in the immaturity of the Bart mode. It needs to grow up and take responsibility for itself.

We've been hit hard with a sudden onslaught of sexual child abuse and we have to deal with it. This isn't television. This isn't a video game. This is real life. We have to protect our little ones.

The 21st Century plague - sexual child abuse

Child molestation is nothing new. It's been around since the dawn of time, rotting the fabric of society. Until recently it has been discussed only in whispers, but in the past 10 years, newspapers have become more and more filled with stories of the sexual assault of children.

Why? What's going on?

Several things.

Pedophiles used to live like solitary moles, furtively looking at obscene photos of children in the dark corners of their lives. They had no one to talk to about their interests because they were too shameful.

Suddenly, the advent of the Internet gave them a forum for discussion with other like minded predators. Where the soul destroying pictures were once so difficult to procure, millions of images of depravity suddenly became available with the click of a mouse.

There's strength in numbers. Reinforcement brought an increased boldness. Child molesters began trading images and videoing scenes of the sexual abuse of children, brainwashing themselves into thinking they were some kind of an oppressed minority group.

Michael Brière was the 36-year-old computer programmer who raped, murdered and dismembered beautiful 10-year-old Holly Jones in Toronto in 2003. Holly had simply been walking home from a friend's house and innocently passed Brière's house on the way. Unbeknownst to anyone, he had been looking at child pornography on the Web and had begun to have fantasies about having sex with a child. After a couple of years of indulging in his "dark secret," he became consumed with the idea. "I really wanted to have sex with a child. And that was all consuming. I just came out of my place and she was just there." For the sake of 40 minutes of indulging his darkest fantasy, Brière lost his place in the world and Holly was lost to the world.

Sexual abuse of children is becoming epidemic in our society, as will become apparent throughout this book. Whatever the sources or motivations, children are being used and abused in alarming numbers. Things have to change. We have to find ways to keep them safe and clean up the moral air we breathe.

We, as a society, need a paradigm shift.

Oprah's next job

Among all the opportunities available to Oprah Winfrey to pursue after ending the "Oprah Show," she once claimed she would become an activist against child sex-offenders. Having been abused in childhood, she has journeyed to the dark places of the soul of an abused child. She knows about the damage inflicted in the hidden places and vowed to devote her life to making sure that abusers pay heavily for their crimes against children.

Until recent years, no one talked about child molestation. Pedophiles hid in the shame they brought on their victims. With all the hoopla surrounding high profile cases and sad revelations like those of the Mount Cashel Orphanage, sexual abuse has slowly emerged from the shadows of shame to revelations of reality. Now people are talking and victims are beginning to understand that they have nothing to be ashamed of. The shame belongs only to the perpetrator.

While the spotlight on the Michael Jackson case (whether warranted or not) and others gradually faded, the increased awareness of the crisis of child sexual abuse has risen like a giant mushroom spawned from mould. But what do we do with it?

We have to understand the impact that it has on those who are molested, the *pornographication*[1] of society, the consequences of failing to protect children and the way victims can find healing.

And then there's the problem of the offenders. What do we do with them on a long-term basis? Oprah's plan seems to be to round them up, slam the iron doors and throw away the keys. For violent, repeat offenders, that's a no brainer. However, as a just society, we condemn a criminal to a proscribed prison term and then, after serving the time, he or she is released—usually having lost everything required to try to reshape his or

1. My new word, meaning, "the conversion of an individual, group or society from normalcy, modesty and decency to acceptance of writings, pictures, films and behavior (usually considered obscene) intended primarily to arouse lustful sexual desire."

her life. What do we do with pedophiles to make sure they don't re-offend? Do we require them to wear a scarlet "P" on their shirts? Do we march in front of their homes until they give up trying to redeem themselves and sink into recidivism? Or is there another, smarter solution? (See "Smart Justice" - Chapter Eight)

Who says what is right or wrong?

While there have been cultures, such as the ancient Greeks, which have sanctioned adult child sex, there's always been a schizophrenic underbelly to the lifestyle. Greek poetry abounds with references to men swooning for "the tender flower of youth and the thighs and delicious mouth of pubescent boys...but we hear nothing from youths admiring the hairy thighs and bristling lips of their bearded lovers."[2]

Nowhere was the schizophrenic attitude towards sex more evident than in Victorian London of the 19th century. While even whispers of sex were taboo and the anti-sensual mind-set was so prudish that gentlemen would even cover the legs of their pianos, there was a population of 80,000 prostitutes in a total population of about two million people.[3]

Let's be clear and disallow this schizophrenia to characterize our society today.

There is no group of children, anywhere in the world, asking to be allowed to have sex with adults. Adult-child sex—sexual

2. Rush, F. (1980). *The Best Kept Secret: Sexual Abuse of Children*. New York, McGraw-Hill Book Company, p.52.
3. The Lancet Medical Journal (1887), from an article by Is'haq Modibbo Kawu in the Nigerian Daily Trust (Aug. 16, 2007).

child abuse—is an adult offense against the most vulnerable members of society.

While one might expect C.S. Lewis, Ravi Zacharias, Deepak Chopra or other religious apologists to argue for right or wrong according to the Bible or the Koran or whatever moral code book they follow, they all recognize that there is a standard, independent of culture, underlying the framework of all mankind. Philosophical arguments of ethics become meaningless apart from the recognition of this unchanging standard that guides human nature.[4]

So it's not up to us to decide what's right or wrong. That has already been written into the DNA of mankind. No matter how acceptable moral relativism may become in any circles, when it contravenes the absolutes of the underlying standard of morality of humanity, society won't function properly.

Anyone hanging wallpaper knows about a plumb line. No matter how crooked a wall may be, when one hangs the plumb line, it becomes immediately apparent where the edge of the paper needs to go. Otherwise, the patterns will never be right. It's the same with morality. No matter how moral relativism may try to skew right or wrong, when the universal, unchanging standard of morality is applied, dysfunctions disappear.

We must never tolerate the sexual abuse of children under the guise of tolerating cultural or ethical diversity. It's just wrong. Period.

---

4. Hergenhahn, B.R. (1992). *An Introduction to the History of Psychology*. Belmont, CA: Wadsworth Publishing Company and Singer, P. (1991). Ethics. *The New Encyclopedia Britannica*, Volume 18, Edition 15, p. 492-521

Child sex abuse defined

In order to understand and study the problem effectively, so that we can figure out how to eradicate it, we have to have universal consensus on exactly what constitutes child sexual abuse.

At present, each state in the U.S. has its own definitions of child abuse based on minimum standards set by Federal law. Other countries all have their own definitions. The Public Health Agency of Canada has defined it clearly:

> "(It) occurs when a child is used for sexual purposes by an adult or adolescent. It involves exposing a child to any sexual activity or behavior. Sexual abuse most often involves fondling and may include inviting a child to touch or be touched sexually. Other forms of sexual abuse include sexual intercourse, juvenile prostitution and sexual exploitation through child pornography. Sexual abuse is inherently emotionally abusive and is often accompanied by other forms of mistreatment. It is a betrayal of trust and is an abuse of power over the child."[5]

In order to qualify as sexual abuse, an activity must have three elements:

- The violation of a trust relationship with unequal power and/or advanced knowledge (and)
- The need for secrecy (and)
- Sexual activity. [6]

By applying these three criteria, it can be determined whether or

---

5. Public Health Agency of Canada (2007), National Clearinghouse on Family Violence.
6. Groth, N., Burgess, A., Birnbaum, H. and Gary, T. (1978). A study of the child molester. Myths and realities. *LAE Journal of the American Criminal Justice Association*, 41(1), Winter/Spring, p. 17-22.

not questionable activity should qualify as abuse. For instance, if children (with equal power) engage in light sexual exploration before the age of puberty, it's generally safe to assume that the behavior is part of normal development and doesn't require legal intervention.

Prevalence

While the prevalence and incidents of child sexual abuse varies around the world, there is nowhere that it does not exist.

Because not all victims report their abuse, not all offenders are caught and some allegations are false – it is impossible to know, definitively, how widespread the problem is. Canadian studies suggest that 19 out of 20 cases are unreported. American statistics show that 67 percent of sexual assaults are committed against children and teenagers. Of those, 34 percent involve children under the age of 12.

Another difficulty with trying to ascertain the actual prevalence is that different researchers with different definitions in different types of population groups ask different questions through different means—such as via telephone, face-to-face or written questionnaires. These differences can affect results.

Further, according to Dr. J. Hopper who has done extensive research in the field,

> "Any research study, even one with the most effective methodology, is likely to underestimate the actual prevalence of sexual abuse in the population being investigated. There is evidence coming to light that as many as one in three incidents

> of child sexual abuse are not remembered by adults who experienced them, and that the younger the child was at the time of the abuse, and the closer the relationship to the abuser, the more likely one is not to remember."[7]

Combining these research gathering issues with the fact that it is impossible to get information on every instance of abuse, one has to conclude that actual figures are impossible to determine.

The only conclusion is that the studies

> "clearly confirm sexual abuse to be an international problem."[8]

Until recent years, there was very little written about the subject because it was regarded as a relatively rare aberration—a taboo. In the 1970s, however, it began to show up in more and more studies as a contributing factor in all kinds of emotional, relational and behavioral disturbances. A nationwide study in the United States found a 600 percent rise in the number of reported cases from 1976 to 1982![9] In Britain, reports of abuse rose from seven in 1977 to 527 by 1986.[10]

Julian Sher, author of *One Child at a Time*, tells the story of Paul Griffiths, an officer in Manchester, England, who was engaged in tackling sex crimes. In the 10 years between 1990 and 2000, issues dealing with child obscenity rose from three to 87 percent of his unit's cases. The rise was credited to the

---

7. Hopper, Dr. J. (2007). Child Abuse: Statistics, Research and Resources, p.23
8. Finkelhor, D. (1994). The International epidemiology of child sexual abuse. *Child Abuse & Neglect*, 18, 409-417
9. Finkelhor, D. (1984). *Child Sexual Abuse: New Theory and Research*, New York: Free Press in Colton, Matthew and Vanstone, Maurice (1996). *Betrayal of Trust*; Sexual Abuse by Men Who Work With Children, , London ON: Free Association Books Ltd., p. 2.
10. Birchall, E. (1989). The Frequency of Child Abuse—What do We Really Know?, in Colton, Matthew and Vanstone, Maurice (1996). *Betrayal of Trust*; Sexual Abuse by Men Who Work With Children, , London ON: Free Association Books Ltd., p.2.

sudden availability of child pornography via the Internet, which started to be used by the general public in 1992.

While it is now generally accepted that one in four women and one in six to ten men have been abused in childhood,[11] other, more recent studies suggest that the numbers are considerably higher. From 2005 information supplied by the Public Health Agency of Canada, the most extensive study of child sexual abuse in Canada was conducted by the Committee on Sexual Offences Against Children and Youths. The results of the report revealed that 53 percent of Canadian women and 31 percent of Canadian men were sexually abused as children. That means that, according to this report, in any representative lineup at a football stadium, theatre or grocery store, about half of the women and a third of the men have experienced some kind of sexual abuse as children!

But it gets worse. In 2006, Angela Shelton, a Hollywood screenwriter, model and actress, produced a multi-award winning documentary called "Searching for Angela Shelton." Her goal was to meet other Angela Sheltons in America and survey women in the US. As she began meeting other Angelas, she found that 70 percent had been victims of rape, childhood sexual assault and/or domestic violence.

In 2006, the United Nations released the first "UN Secretary General's Study on Violence against Children." It was the first comprehensive, global study conducted by the UN on all forms of violence against children. It revealed that:

---

11. Van Dam, Carla (2001). *Identifying Child Molesters, Preventing Child Sexual Abuse by Recognizing the Patterns of the Offenders,* New York: The Halworth Maltreatment and Trauma Press, p.75.

- Almost 53,000 children died worldwide in 2002 as a result of homicide.
- 150 million girls and 73 million boys under 18 experienced forced sexual intercourse or other forms of sexual violence during 2002.
- Estimates from 2000 suggest that 1.8 million children were forced into prostitution and pornography and 1.2 million were victims of trafficking.[12]

While the study engaged directly with children, providing opportunities for them to participate in all regional consultations, describing both their experiences and their proposals for ending the abuse, the figures are, at best, estimates, because so much that happens in secret is kept in secret.

A medical article on child abuse was published in the June, 2007 edition of the *Malta Medical Journal*, written by pediatricians Dr. Simon Attard Montalto and Dr. Mariella Mangion. In it, they stated that the "worrying" increase in figures of child abuse cannot be explained away by improved medical diagnosis or increased awareness. The reasons given for the increasing numbers included,

> "disintegration of social protective barriers, family fragmentation, increase in unwanted babies, pressures of parenting, daily stress, and crime—especially associated with illegal drug use."

Efforts to determine a realistic estimate of the magnitude of the problem are increasingly complicated by estranged couples

12. UN Secretary General's Study on Violence Against Children (2006) section II.B., pp.9-10

fabricating claims of abuse on their offspring by their ex-partner, thereby using the children as pawns in their battles.

We have to kick it up a few notches for our kids. All of the above reasons are based on some form of individual selfishness, bad choices and immaturity. These numbers could come down with each person making the individual choice in the quiet of his or her own home, to grow up and live differently. That's not a statement of judgement. It's a statement of recognition that little ones around the world can be protected from a lifetime of pain if we just reach out to help ease the stresses of others rather than always reaching inward to look after ourselves.

Some known consequences of child sexual abuse

Because only a percentage of actual incidents are reported, it is impossible to ascertain the full impact on society or on individuals. According to the American Medical Association, one-fifth of all victims of child sexual abuse develop serious, long-term psychological problems. The following list is simply an attempt to identify some of the known results and is not meant to suggest that any individual will suffer all of the results listed.

- Post-traumatic stress disorder
- Increased drug and alcohol abuse
- Obsessive-compulsive disorder
- Panic attacks and anxiety disorders
- Depression
- Personality disorders
- Increased utilization of health services
- Increased utilization of social services

- Sexual dysfunctions - ranging from sex addiction to total aversion to sex
- Suicidal ideation
- Greater risk for relationship and parenting problems[13]

That's the obvious list. Less obvious are the rampant psychosomatic disorders that can't be definitively linked to the abuse—headaches, lower back problems and muscle tension caused by stress.

Day to day life for an abuse survivor can be filled with the residue of the experience. Gone is the opportunity for normal peer exploration. Victims already know all about "it." Relationships can no longer happen normally. The secrecy inherent in all abuse situations robs the child of normal intimacy with anyone—because he or she has a secret which must be guarded at all costs. No one else can get close. The child lives in emotional isolation, often so preoccupied with thoughts of the secret, that it is impossible to concentrate on other normal tasks like school and goal setting. Unable to understand why the child doesn't focus or get more involved with those around him or her, people can get frustrated with the child, further alienating him or her from normal, loving relationships.

The normal attachment issues are complicated by an inability to properly regulate emotions and stress response.

Self-esteem issues can be huge as survivors grapple with the understanding of their value. It's very difficult to know you've

13. Van Dam, Carla (2001). *Identifying Child Molesters, Preventing Child Sexual Abuse by Recognizing the Patterns of the Offenders*, New York: The Halworth Maltreatment and Trauma Press, p. 60.

been used like a toy or consumed like a piece of meat. If that sense of not having as much value as other people is not put in perspective, seeing the offender as the one who is "not like other people," victims can spiral downwards into a life of chronic victimization, allowing themselves to be further used by other people. Finding clear perspective is critical.

Children who have been abused and have not found recovery, are more likely to stay in abusive relationships. Having developed the pattern of putting up with pain and unhappiness in childhood, they have established a kind of perverse "comfort zone." It's a situation of damsels (or boys) in distress feeling as though things are most familiar in the distress—the painful "known" versus the peaceful "unknown." Exiting from such a situation successfully, requires the individual to make the emotional transition from the helplessness of a child to the recognition of empowered adulthood.

The inability to trust is generally the central issue as abused children grow into adulthood. A child who has been abused by an adult in a position of trust, such as a father, grandfather or priest may have a hard time ever trusting again. This inability to trust ripples out to include everyone surrounding the child during the time of the abuse because they (knowingly or unknowingly) failed to protect him or her. And then there's the issue of trusting themselves to know whom to trust. If they make a mistake, they risk being used or rejected again—like a china doll left broken, abandoned on the floor with a cracked head.

At the very least, sexual abuse of children most often results in bitterness, hostility, misplaced guilt, depression and shame.

Unless properly addressed and dealt with, these can last a lifetime, destroying not just the lives of the victims, but all those whose lives are entwined with them. This will be further discussed in Chapter Seven.

Maintaining perspective

Having touched on many of the known consequences of child sexual abuse, it is important not to exaggerate the effects. Everyone reacts differently to circumstances. In their writings on the initial and long-term effects of sexual child abuse, Browne and Finkelhor[14] warned about over exaggeration. While the mental health industry has described child sexual abuse as "a special destroyer of adult mental health," their conclusions are largely based on clinical samples and so are not necessarily representative. If that contention were true and the latest findings that indicate that over half of the female population of the world and a third of the males have been abused, a huge segment of our society would be exhibiting destruction of their mental health. That's just not so. Destruction of mental health is not necessarily a consequence of child sexual abuse.

At the other end of the continuum, we have a pile of studies indicating that child sexual abuse results in little psychological harm. The advocates of adult-child sex, while obviously in the minority, are becoming more and more vocal and can easily skew studies to bolster their agenda.

To me, it's simply a no-brainer that something as unnatural and

14. Browne, A., & Finkelhor, D. (1986). Initial and long-term effects: A review of the research. In D. Finkelhor, A Sourcebook on Child Sexual Abuse (pp. 143-179). Beverly Hills: Sage.

traumatic as child molestation (no matter how gentle or sadistic) is going to affect a developing child—but to varying degrees, depending on the individual and individual circumstances.

Abuse add-ons

Sexual abuse seldom happens in isolation. A study of 17,421 adults at Kaiser Permanente's Department of Preventative Medicine in San Diego found that of the adults who reported being sexually abused as children, many of them reported other traumatic experiences that were happening concurrently—things like neglect, losing a parent as a result of divorce or imprisonment, living with a dysfunctional parent who was a substance abuser.

This is particularly interesting when coupled with the knowledge that child molesters often seek out needy children.

Those in the study who had at least four adverse factors going on were twice as likely to be smokers, 12 times more likely to have committed suicide, seven times more likely to be alcoholics and 10 times more likely to use street drugs. Dr. Vincent Felitti, one of the authors of *The Adverse Childhood Experience Study* wrote:

> "The study makes it clear that time does not heal some of the adverse experience we found so common in the childhoods of a large population of middle-aged, middle class Americans. One does not "just get over some things, not even 50 years later."[15]

15. The San Francisco Chronicle (April 3, 2005).

Economic factors

When we fail in our efforts to protect children, there is a cost beyond the trauma to the individual and his or her family and friends. Economic costs for child welfare services as well as the indirect costs of the long-term consequences of abuse, take a toll on the economy of individuals, families and nations.

Sadly, the understanding of child sexual abuse as a priority has failed to reach the budget pencils of those who hold the purse strings.

A 2001 study by the Edna McConnell Clark Foundation used federal data to determine annual direct costs of all child abuse in the United States, including medical, police, welfare and court costs. The figure was 24 billion dollars. With an estimated 20 percent of abuse being sexual in nature, the known U.S. federal costs were, at that time, around five billion dollars. With numbers constantly climbing and so many cases unreported, the numbers are obviously much higher—to say nothing of the familial costs of dealing with an abused child and the costs to the business world for workers who continue to suffer with emotional baggage.

According to Dr. Paul Fink,

> "Child sexual abuse is a preventable health problem that has been allowed to spread, unabated, due to scientific and social neglect."[16]

Dr. Frank Putnam, researcher at the National Institute for Mental Health, in his article, *Why is it so Difficult for the Epidemic of Child Abuse to be Taken Seriously?* observed,

16. Fink, Paul (2005). *Science*, Vol. 309, August.

"We find an incidence rate for child abuse and neglect that is about ten times as high as the incidence rate for all forms of cancer. . . . There is a multi-billion-dollar research base reliably renewed on an annual basis for cancer treatment and prevention. Nothing remotely similar to this exists for child abuse and neglect."

It's probably worth noting that there's no pill that the mammoth drug companies could produce to stop child abuse or its effects. As a crisis control driven society, rather than a prevention oriented society, there may be money to be saved, but none to be made. Money spent on preventing sexual child abuse would not produce any direct financial return on investment.

In a commentary, Dr. James Mercy, a researcher with the Center for Disease Control and Prevention observed:

"Imagine a childhood disease that affects one in five girls and one in seven boys before they reach 18 (Finkelhor & Dziuba-Leatherman, 1994): a disease that can cause dramatic mood swings, erratic behavior, and even severe conduct disorders among those exposed; a disease that breeds distrust of adults and undermines the possibility of experiencing normal sexual relationships; a disease that can have profound implications for an individual's future health by increasing the risk of problems such as substance abuse, sexually transmitted diseases, and suicidal behavior (Crowell & Burgess, 1996); a disease that replicates itself by causing some of its victims to expose future generations to its debilitating effects.

"Imagine what we, as a society, would do if such a disease existed. We would spare no expense. We would invest heavily in basic and applied research. We would devise systems to identify those affected and provide services to treat them. We would develop and broadly implement prevention campaigns to protect our children. Wouldn't we?

"Such a disease does exist—it's called child sexual abuse. Our response, however, has been far from the full-court press reserved for traditional diseases or health concerns of equal or even lesser magnitude. Perhaps the perception of sexual abuse as a law enforcement problem or our discomfort in confronting sexual issues contributes to our complacency. Whatever the reason, we have severely underestimated the effects of this problem on our children's health and quality of life."[17]

Denial

So—if the costs are so high, why don't we do more to get at the root of the problem?

People don't want to talk about child sexual abuse, much less admit to being a victim or a molester. People don't want to look too closely or they might find something horrible going on next door or even in their own homes. The problem is so rampant that, for many social workers, dealing with the subject means confronting their own childhood demons. They don't want to stir their own emotional pots, bringing their buried painful, sometimes shameful memories to the surface.

---

17. Mercy, J. A. (1999). Having New Eyes: Viewing Child Sexual Abuse as a Public Health Problem. Sexual Abuse: A Journal of Research and Treatment, 11(4), 317-321.

The word "incest" is so distasteful that people want to distance themselves from it in every way—even in the development of sex abuse prevention programs, which are predominantly geared towards strangers. Author Julian Sher's research into the findings of the CCRC (Crimes Against Children Research Centre, University of New Hampshire) revealed that between 70 and 90 percent of child sexual abuse is committed by persons known to the victim.

This societal denial is another factor contributing to inadequate funding for the development of programs geared to protecting kids. People in positions of intimacy with children, such as teachers, doctors and nurses, who have opportunities to check for signs of abuse are usually poorly trained in recognizing the more subtle signs.

According to Victor Vieth, director of the American Prosecutors Research Institute's National Centre for Prosecution of Child Abuse, a 2004 survey of 2,240 judges who regularly handle child abuse cases, showed that barely 50 percent had had the proper training. Consequently, children who should be rescued continue to be either abused or at risk. He states:

> "All the folks who advocate getting tough on crime and other social problems—burglaries, arsons, suicide, depression—need to start talking about addressing child abuse, because that's where much of it starts."

Known incidents—the tip of the iceberg

Counselors on the front lines of the epidemic of child sexual abuse know that incarcerated sex offenders are only the tip of the iceberg in terms of the proportion of active sex offenders.

Most incidents of child sex abuse are never reported—for a variety of reasons.

- Fear of retaliation by the offender—Many offenders control their victims with threats.
- Fear of not being believed—Particularly in cases where the abuser is highly respected in the family or community, the victim often fears that he or she will not be believed.
- The shame of things done in secret—It's embarrassing to have people know what one has done on an intimate level.
- The shame of enjoyment—Not all touches by an offender are distasteful to a child. Knowing that what is happening is wrong and yet finding occasional pleasure in the relationship makes a child feel ashamed of himself/herself.
- Love for the offender—Offenders are sometimes dearly loved family members who shamefully confuse children with loving touches combined with inappropriate touches.
- Protection of the family—It's not uncommon for a child to fear that they will ruin their families if they tell.
- Fear of the ordeal of testifying—The thought of facing one's abuser in court can be overwhelming. In trying to protect their children from further damage, parents often try to sidestep the court process and deal with the situation the best way they know how.
- Fear of peer group reaction—"What will my friends think of me if I tell?"

- Deer in the headlights—It's not uncommon for a victim to "freeze" like a deer in the headlights, when abuse occurs. The traumatic experience paralyzes them in terms of ability to seek help.
- Confusion—Little children do not have the same frames of reference as adults. They do not process things the same way. They don't have the life experiences necessary to know how things will play out. Living between an offender who is instructing him to be silent and a parent who is teaching him or her to be vocal about bad touches can be a very confusing place for a child.
- Attempts by the family at cover-up—It is not uncommon for a wife who does not have her own resources and who is entirely dependant on her husband, to believe the promises of the offender that he will stop offending and not report the abuse.

In the words of sexual abuse specialist Roland C. Summit,

> "In the classic role reversal of child abuse, the child is given the power to destroy the family and the responsibility to keep it together. The child, not the parent, must mobilize the altruism and self-control to insure the survival of the others. The child, in short, must secretly assume many of the role-functions ordinarily assigned to the mother.
>
> "There is an inevitable splitting of conventional moral values. Maintaining a lie to keep the secret is the ultimate virtue, while telling the truth would be the greatest sin. A child thus victimized will appear to accept or to seek sexual contact without complaint."

A child is *never, never* to be regarded as complicit in sexual abuse. As Dr. David Finkelhor, a psychologist at the University of New Hampshire who has written extensively on the subject of child sexual abuse, states,

> "For true consent to occur, two conditions must prevail. A person must know what it is that he or she is consenting to and a person must be free to say yes or no."

Obviously, children do not have the capacity to give consent.

Incest—the family secret

Until recently, when people began to open up about childhood secrets, it was thought that incest (where the offender is a member of one's own family or someone in a very close position of trust—such as a stepfather or stepmother) was a disgusting, rare aberration, most commonly found in the hills of Kentucky.

Disgusting, yes—but rare, no—and Kentucky, yes, but everywhere else, too.

A Canadian Public Health Agency fact sheet revealed that:

> "Incest offenders reflect the same range of education, religion, occupation, intelligence and mental health status as can be found in a representative cross-section of the general population. Abusers are found among all ages, ethnocultural communities and social classes."

Once again, because of the nature of the crime, exact statistics are impossible to gather. The FBI and the U.S. Justice Department estimate that only one in ten cases is reported. Still, from their work in the field, Susan Forward and Craig Buck[18] estimate that ten million American women have been incest victims, while Sandra Butler[19] contends that the figure is closer to twenty-five million.

Whatever the true numbers are, they are staggering, when one considers the betrayal of trust behind each and every one of those numbers.

> "Incest is perhaps the most difficult kind of abuse for children to endure, because the feelings it generates are so overwhelming, confusing and conflicting. Children instinctively love their parents and other family members and cannot reconcile this love with what is being done to them. They are torn between love and hate, and tormented by the betrayal of those they trusted. They are overwhelmed by helplessness because they cannot escape; they have nowhere to go. The very people to whom they should run for protection are their abusers. And they believe that if they tell, they will destroy their families and their source of survival. They are trapped and helpless. And they are tortured by the conviction that they are bad or evil and that they are somehow to blame.[20]
>
> "As if the natural attachment were not enough to immobilize victims, psychologists have recently discovered that the abusive situation itself establishes a bond between abuser and victim.

18. Forward, Susan, and Craig Buck (1979). *Betrayal of Innocence: Incest and its Devastation,* New York: Penguin Books.
19. Butler, Sandra (1985). *Conspiracy of Silence: The Trauma of Incest,* San Francisco, Volcano Press.
20. Finney, Lynne D. (1992). *Reach for the Rainbow*; Advanced Healing for Survivors of Sexual Abuse, New York: The Putnam Publishing Group, p.35

> This bond chains the victim to the abuser even if the abuser is completely unrelated to the victim. This grim phenomenon is known as the "Stockholm Syndrome," and it was first detected in hostage situations where hostages were found to experience positive feelings towards their captors and negative feelings toward the police. The captors (perpetrators) reciprocated by developing positive feelings towards the hostages. This syndrome is more likely to develop in hostage (or abuse) situations which last for a prolonged period of time.... If the abuse is occurring to a child within the family, the victim is effectively a hostage, without means of escape."[21]

If exhibiting the symptoms of the Stockholm Syndrome, a child may appear to be very affectionate towards the abuser, but it's generally because he or she is trying to exert some control over his or her life. Such children think that if they are particularly pleasing to the perpetrator, the abuse may end or at least their world may not fall apart any more than it already has.

A prevalent myth

Many people are under the illusion that child sexual abuse simply involves fondling (as though fondling isn't a big deal). The reality is quite different.

In the inquiry into the Mount Cashel Orphanage in Newfoundland in 1989, the victims testified that they had been fondled in the showers and beds, and some had also been subjected to sexual acts including fellatio and sodomy. Several spoke of severe physical abuse. According to John McIsaac, a former resident,

21. Butler, Sandra (1985). *Conspiracy of Silence: The Trauma of Incest*, San Francisco, Volcano Press, p. 126.

"If you went along with the sexual acts, the physical beatings weren't going to happen as much."[22]

In a survey of the crimes committed by child molesters referred to a Massachusetts forensic mental health clinic, it was found that 39 percent were confined to fondling or masturbation, but 31 percent involved oral, anal or vaginal penetration and 13 percent involved both. No data were available for 17 percent of the subjects of the study.[23]

A Kingston, Ontario father who sodomized his two-year-old son was so brutal that the child had to be surgically fitted with a colostomy bag.[24]

A study by the Kingston Sexual Behavior Clinic of 150 incarcerated sex offenders showed that 58 percent of child molesters used force beyond what was necessary to commit their crimes.[25]

The Canadian Incidence Study of Reported Child Abuse and Neglect in 2001 reported that "attempted and completed sexual activity accounted for over one-third (35 percent) of all substantiated reports of sexual abuse."

Even when the behavior of an offender may be gentle or cajoling at first, study after study shows that the activity and the use of force or coercion usually accelerates as the molestation continues. When a child molester gets away with his abuse for a period of time, it appears that he gains confidence, a sense of invulnerability and a sense of power over the victims.

22. Marshall, Dr. W.L. and Barrett, Sylvia (1990). *Criminal Neglect*; Why Sex Offenders Go Free, Toronto: Doubleday Canada Limited, p. 93-94
23. Ibid, p. 93
24. Ibid, p. 93
25. Ibid, p. 94

What are they *THINKING?*

Aberrant thoughts that would never before have dared to form themselves into spoken words, much less public discussion, have now grown into foundational philosophies for a sector of groups that openly preach that sexual activity with children is wholesome. They use slogans like, "Sex before eight or else it's too late." Styling themselves a "sexual minority," they dare to demand civil rights to legitimize their sexual preference (which is, of course, criminal behavior).

No matter how decent human beings may rant about the ridiculousness of such ideas, internet child pornography traffic indicates that this perspective is growing at an alarming rate.

Some are calling it "pedophilia chic." I can barely write this, it is so nauseating.

Until recently, the taboo against using young boys to satisfy adult sex appetites was no less controversial than bestiality. It was "wrong" right across the board. Anyone who thought otherwise was regarded as the lowest of the low.

However, things are changing. In certain circles where sex with little boys is considered to be the new frontier, it's regarded as being edgy.

Amazingly, this criminal activity is showing up for discussion by so-called "respected" academicians and physicians in academic and literary circles as well as mainstream journals and magazines.

For instance, the *Journal of American Medical Association* published a paper in 2002 by Peter J. Fagan, Ph.D., et al. titled "Pedophilia." Consider the following quote from the article:

> "During psychosexual development, no one decides whether to be attracted to women, men, *girls or boys*. Rather, individuals discover the types of persons they are sexually attracted to, i.e., their sexual orientation." (italics added)

While I have not found any evidence to suggest that there is any more relation between homosexuality and pedophilia than there is between heterosexuality and pedophilia, the move towards legitimization of pedophilia as a sexual preference bears similarities to the homosexual movement in the late 1960s.

While this writing is not a commentary on homosexuality, this new movement to view pedophiles as a legitimate minority is alarming, considering the success of the same tactics which resulted in the explosion of homosexual acceptance. Homosexuals have turned society upside-down regarding a behavior that was once viewed just as perverse as pedophilia by the majority. Now, the term "sexual orientation" in relation to pedophilia is being used more and more. The same arguments that gay activists used to gain acceptance for their behavior are no doubt the same arguments that will be used to try to justify pedophilia as normal.

While we might have hoped the underlying current was just for temporary shock value, there appears to be more to the issue.

It appears that the more the gay rights movement moves into the mainstream, the more the discussion is raised. The attempts to legitimize sex with children never seems to be about little girls. It's always about little boys. There's no adult/child "love association" for little girls: only the adult/child "love association" for little boys.

It goes without saying that many gay men are disgusted by the idea and want nothing but consensual adult sex – however, others in the movement differ, a situation mirrored in the heterosexual community.

The gay rights movement boasts some of the most successful lobbyists / activists since the Cold War. Their unrelenting determination has turned what was regarded 20 years ago as a societal aberration, into a legitimized segment of society. As their movement grew dramatically, several national gay rights groups tried to gain respectability by denouncing the groups advocating sex with children. However, the attitude was not across the board. In 1996, J. Gallagher and C. Bull came out with a pro-movement book, *Perfect Enemies: The Religious Right, the Gay Movement, and the Politics of the 1990s*, in which they attempted to explain the difficulty of denouncing these groups because,

> "many thoughtful activists who opposed ------'s goals could not escape the suspicion that to denounce the organization would be to mimic society's condemnation of their own sexual orientation."

Portrayals of "inter-generational sex" here and there in gay literature doesn't help the movement in their attempts to be regarded as respectable. It sets them back, because respectable, character-oriented society will never tolerate the exploitation of precious children for sexual purposes. That's where the line is drawn. For whatever the reasons, instead of standing firmly against child sexual abuse with the rest of society, the gay rights movement seems to be divided.

The slide towards tolerance of child sex abuse appears to be methodically designed to filter into mainstream thought.

There was an article in the Psychological Bulletin (1998) called, "A Meta-Analytic Examination of Assumed Properties of Child Sexual Abuse Using College Samples," coauthored by Bruce Rind, Robert Bauserman and Philip Tromovitch. Full of polished professional jargon, the point was that the ideas about negative effects of child sexual abuse were overblown, particularly with male children. Further, they suggested that the terms, "victim" and "perpetrator" be dropped in situations of consensual sexual activity between men and boys and that those encounters would simply be referred to as "adult-child sex."

Another manipulative thrust of the article was the comparison of pedophilia to things like masturbation, homosexuality and sexual promiscuity "which were codified as pathological in the first edition of the American Psychiatric Association's (1952) *Diagnostic and Statistical Manual of Mental Disorders*," and are no longer codified—suggesting that pedophilia should be the next behavior to be decodified.

One molester pointed out that, "the taboo against sex with children is Victorian-age hysteria whipped up by feminists who don't understand male sexuality." He states, "all the harm is done by the taboo. If nobody is getting hurt, there is nothing to worry about."[26]

While the Rind article was essentially a rehashing of the previous twenty years of efforts to vindicate homosexual pedophilia, it

26. Van Dam, Carla (2001). *Identifying Child Molesters, Preventing Child Sexual Abuse by Recognizing the Patterns of the Offenders*, New York: The Halworth Maltreatment and Trauma Press, p. 58.

gained notoriety and wider legitimacy (in certain circles) simply through its degree of exposure.

Why all the fuss?

The mindset of many in our society has had a paradigm shift. We're living in a different world and our children, the ones who depend on us to protect them, are like sitting ducks – at the mercy of the shifting mindset. The world is no longer a safe place for them without our focused attention on their care.

That's why all the fuss.

Who is the Predator?

Who can know the darkness of heart that dwells within anyone? Until outed through charges being laid against them, predators are usually impossible to spot. They lurk behind masks designed to look like everyman or everywoman.

My research was not limited to libraries or news reports. I gained valuable insight from individuals who were willing to expose their hearts in interviews in hopes that their sharing would assist in the battle to protect children.

One of these contributors was Matt, a middle-aged professional man who lost his wife, family, home, profession, reputation, dignity, friends and total sense of worth when charged and convicted of molesting two young girls. While not an example of a sadistic pedophile, he is typical of a multitude of predators who started out dabbling in pornography and ended up destroying the lives around them and losing everything.

We met one cold, fall morning. I plugged in my equipment to record the sad legacy of this man's life. He was broken and totally open to exposing his deepest shame if it could in any way dissuade anyone thinking of targeting a child from acting on fantasies, or if it could in any way bring healing, insight or prevention into the epidemic of child molestation.

D. Let's go back to the beginning. Where did this all start? What was the root?

M. Pornography was certainly a major contributing factor.

D. Was there anything else at the root of it?

M. Well, the absence of a healthy adult sexual relationship was not a good environment for me to be in.

D. How do you account for that? What was wrong with your relationship with your wife?

M. I think that on our honeymoon when I was more open about wanting to do the kind of stuff I saw in pornography, and I realized that she wasn't into it, I disconnected and took the easy way out in more pornography and fantasizing and other relationships. We just grew apart. Instead of working on a healthy relationship, I replaced normal, healthy sex with more and more degrading pornography.

D. So you had no desire for normal sex ?

M. No.

D. Do you think that if your wife had participated in all the things you wanted to do that you would never have gotten involved with the first young girl?

M. There's no way of knowing that. I never had any thoughts of kids. All the time I was messing around with other women while I was travelling so much, it was all about adults. The thought of kids never crossed my mind.

D. In terms of the root, do you feel that there was anything generational, or anything in you that led you to be attracted to children? Do you feel that you were born with that sexual predisposition?

M. I don't think so. Psychologists have determined that I am not a real pedophile. Not all people who molest children are pedophiles. True pedophiles just go for kids. That is not my preference. I was always into adult sex but got involved with the two young girls because they were there and I was so selfish that I cared more about self-gratification than anything else at the time. I think that in both cases, with both girls, it was a matter of convenience. I was in a trusted position for a long time.

D. When you were a child, did you have sexual experiences or were you molested by anyone?

M. When I was about nine, I was molested by a counselor at a Scout camp. I called home and tried to get my parents to come and get me, but they didn't and so I told the senior camp counselor. Then my parents came and got me. Other than that, there were about three instances of experimentation with other children who were older that I, but in talking with psychologists, they seem to think that those circumstances were just normal childhood curiosity.

D. What did your parents say to you about it?

M. We never talked about it. It was as though it never happened.

D. Do you feel that had any effect on your sexual development or your relationship with your wife, or...

M. I don't know. It wasn't a good situation. I felt very ostracized at the camp because I was treated like the snitch who had caused this fellow who molested me to be sent home. Everybody was mad because this fellow had been very popular. They didn't know what he had done to me. I just wanted to go home, to get out of there. I was there for about a day before my parents came.

D. Do you, yourself, feel that the incidents with other children were normal childhood occurrences—or do you feel that they had an effect on your development?

M. It's not something that you can qualify. I don't know what I would have been like had those things never happened.

D. Research speaks of the "grooming process" child molesters use to gain the trust of their victims and families. Did you intentionally groom your first victim with the intent of molesting her?

M. While I had begun to fantasize about schoolgirls, I never intended to actually get myself in a situation of molesting a child. The first time it happened, I was leading a children's church group and a young girl who was a foster child of a family in the church used to want to be around me all the time. She had been sexually active in a previous home and was very clingy with any male leader who would pay attention to her. She was mentally and emotionally weak and just wanted someone to love her. She wanted males to love her. One of the other leaders had to have a talk with her foster mother about how she was constantly making plays for the male leaders. I played on her needs. One day when I was at her home, she flipped her top up out of the blue and exposed her breasts to me. That's when I should have just told her to pull her top down and left the situation, but I didn't.

D. Did the foster parents not suspect anything?

M. The girl's foster mother was very observant. I felt she was always on the outlook for the kids because she had had a previous situation where someone was suspected of molesting one of her grandkids and so I never pushed anything, simply because that would have been a red flag to her. I could sense that she was always very protective.

D. Did you ever feel that she had any distrust of you?

M. No. Not at all. In fact it was exactly the opposite. I was very much in a position of trust with the kids.

D. You must have begun to feel very isolated after all that began to happen. You became isolated from people who could have helped you. Can you talk about how that was?

M. It just reinforced the behavior. It made me go deeper into unreality and interact more with the kids than with the adults. It was a real catch-22 situation.

D. How did you see yourself in relation to other people?

M. I always felt that in a funny sort of way I was superior to other people—that I was smart, that I was clever. I was getting away with it. Did I like me? No. But deep down I always felt that I did a good job at a lot of things. I felt that there weren't a lot of people who could do certain things as well as I could do them. Believe it or not, I thought I was spiritually astute. That was a total deception, obviously. I was proud to the extent of being vain. Not a very nice person. I worked at trying to appear to be a nice person, but it was all a sham.

D. How long did that situation with that young girl continue?

M. I'm not exactly sure. She eventually went to another home in Toronto. Then there was a church party of some sort and I volunteered to go to Toronto to pick her up and that's when it ended.

D. Why did it end?

M. Because I took her to a secluded spot on the way and proceeded to molest her and she started to cry. That's when I stopped. I snapped out of it and took her home.

D. There were quite a few years between the first girl and your neighbour's daughter, Linda. Why did you choose Linda?

M. I think Linda was the most vulnerable. She was always very clingy and wanted to be around me. She was at my house a lot with my grandkids. Linda was very bright, but she was emotionally needy because of her circumstances and she craved the attention. Other kids who were strong characters never entered my mind. Never even entered my mind.

D. How old was she when you began to touch her?

M. I think she was about ten.

D. Was she frightened?

M. No, I don't think so. It began as a back rub and just progressed from there. In my mind, she was enjoying the attention. I was obviously rationalizing totally inappropriate behavior. It was totally about self-gratification.

D. So her discomfort wouldn't have stopped you.

M. No. The best thing Linda ever did was to tell, because even though I stopped over a year before she told, I'm convinced that I would have started again at some point.

D. Your desires were progressive, then?

M. Yes. I never went beyond touching the girls with my hands, but towards the end, I was fantasizing about being touched and I know I was moving in that direction.

D. When you were touching them, were you physically aggressive? Did you force yourself on them?

M. I did with Linda. I wasn't violent, but I knew that she didn't want to do certain things and I did.

D. Would you have progressed as far as rape?

M. No, I wouldn't have forced her like that, but if she hadn't cried, I would have gone further and if she had given any inkling of wanting to participate—which I know was a ridiculous thought—I would have gone further. That's just how low my mind had sunk.

D. How old was she then?

M. She would have been twelve or thirteen. But in both cases, with both of the girls, when they cried and said stop, I stopped. I think when they cried, they broke through the veil of being objects to me and became children and that's when I stopped.

D. When you were molesting a child, how did you feel about the child?

M. I didn't really have any... I think I felt that I was giving them pleasure, or that was what I told myself, which was of course not true. It was all about self-gratification. While I was touching them, I really thought of them as objects, not as children. When you're doing that you don't think of them as victims. It's just as though they're nonexistent. They're not people. They're objects.

D. Did you ever have a real relationship with Linda? Was she ever a human being to you—or was she always just an object?

M. Oh no, I cared very deeply for her. It was only when I was trying to self-gratify myself that she was an object. But there were so many times when I felt so close to her. I was almost like a Dr. Jeckyll and Mr. Hyde. I was very deceptive. Extremely deceptive. There are perpetrators who basically target a kid on the street and use violence but that wasn't my thing. It wasn't anything I ever did or would have done. There was always something deep inside of me that said that wasn't ever going to happen.

D. What were your thoughts after you had molested a young girl?

M. Regret. Deep, deep regret. I felt very unworthy. Like a real heel. A real schmuck.

D. So after Linda cried, it never happened again?

M. That's right. It never happened again. And I think it was over a year before she reported me. If I hadn't gotten caught, I know I would have tried again. The victim needs to tell.

D. If she had been questioned, do you think Linda would have told about it earlier?

I think that communication from adults to the child is extremely important. Because I have a feeling that if anybody had sat down with Linda and asked her if everything was okay in the relationship between her and me, I think she would have spoken up and said that there were some things going on. I doubt that she would have said anything to her teachers at school or whatever, but with someone she really had a relationship with, I think she would have said something if she had been asked.

D. Did you ever want to confess—and if you did, what stopped you?

M. Yes, I did, but fear wouldn't let me. I was trapped. There was nothing I could do about it without blowing my family apart—which has happened.

D. According to the research I've done, one of the characteristics of child molesters is that they don't pay attention to normal societal boundaries. Were you aware that you were breaking societal barriers, or did you just not care, or what?

M. I don't think I was aware that I was breaking societal barriers.

D. So you weren't aware that it was improper to go into a child's bedroom?

M. No. Not really. I was much more comfortable with children than with adults. I think it's because with adults you can't be totally open and honest, but with kids you can and I enjoyed that. So it was a lack of maturity. That and the fact that my guilt prevented me from being able to relax with adults.

D. Did you feel you could express yourself more with kids?

M. No, I would draw them out. I wouldn't talk about my deep feelings with them. I would just talk about them.

D. What would have stopped you from touching a child in the first place?

M. If they had said no. Saying no and crying. In both cases, with both of the girls, that was it. That was what stopped it with both of them. Now—will that stop every child molester? No. I don't think so. It's just that I have a soft heart and when reality sunk in that I was hurting this child, then I stopped.

D. Did you ever hear on TV or on the radio about the consequences of molesting a child?

M. All the time.

D. How did that affect you?

M. I'd just quiver and shake inside and be glad that I hadn't gotten caught.

D. But you proceeded anyway. Why?

M. Just lack of self-will. I'd just always make myself think, well, she appears to like it, so... I mean it was delusional, but that's what I did.

D. Did you want to be caught?

M. I wanted to stop. I didn't want to get caught. I just couldn't figure out how to stop.

D. Did you ever try to seek help in any way?

M. Yes. I would constantly pray that the Lord would get me out of it. I knew it was wrong and felt very guilty after the fact, but just wasn't strong enough to stop it.

D. So if you prayed that God would help you to stop, why do you think He didn't?

M. I think it was just a hollow prayer. It just wasn't sincere. My desire for what I was doing was stronger than my desire to stop.

D. How did you hide your sexual preferences all those years?

M. Just by being very manipulative.

D. Did you feel guilt?

M. Yes.

D. How did you handle that?

M. Just tried to put on a brave face—be someone I wasn't. Basically a mask. I couldn't ever really have an in-depth conversation with anybody for fear something would slip. There was no honesty in anything. It was very depressing. I just buried myself in work projects and so I was never really around anybody for long. I just kept working and working so I didn't have to think about it. That was my self-preservation mechanism.

D. Do you think people have to be cautious when they see a strong bond between a man and a child?

M. I think people have to be perceptive—not cautious—perceptive. For instance, I have a bad feeling about a fellow at my church now. There is a woman there who has two young daughters and a boyfriend. They left the church and he took one of the girls with him—not both girls—one girl. To me that was an instant red flag. I wondered why he separated those girls. So I think that if you want to protect a child, you have to watch how things are orchestrated and understand manipulation.

D. When you questioned that, should you have confronted that, or should you have just let them go as you did and hope for the best?

M. I am going to speak to the pastor about it, but I am in a very delicate position in that church. There are certainly people, I would say the majority of people who are spiritually mature, rational people who understand the nature of forgiveness and are giving me a second chance. There are a few, however, who are really upset about me being there. They haven't actually vocalized their concerns to me, but I certainly sense the vibe. They have spoken to the pastor about it, but he's giving me a chance. It's a hard situation.

D. So you feel that in your position you really can't address it. But for someone else who was concerned, do you feel that the fellow should have been challenged?

M. Well, it was with the full approval of the mom. She went out to his car and opened the door for the little girl to get in and then let them go off on their own. I guess that in my situation right now, I'm just paranoid. I could be over reacting to this situation with the mother and her boyfriend, because friends of the pair who seem to be people of good judgement don't appear to have a problem with it. They seem to think it's okay. Anyway, a parent just has to be wise.

D. Did you ever feel that there was any kind of demonic presence influencing you or harassing you?

M.. No. I think Satan gets blamed for a lot of things he doesn't do. This was just totally selfish human nature.

D. What was it like being accused of child molestation?

M. Gut wrenching. My heart stopped. My mind was spinning thinking, well, this won't be that hard to get out of, because there's no hard evidence. That was my initial instinct, but before I admitted that I was guilty, I started realizing that whether I was proven guilty or not, people were going to think I was, because I had been accused. Reality was slow to seep in, but when it did, I started to realize that I had to do the right thing.

D. Describe your experience with the law. What was it like when the police came to the door?

M. Initially I had no idea what was going on, but my heart went into my stomach. They were very professional. I don't think they believed the accusations at all at first, mainly because they were so nice to me. I would have thought that if they had believed it, I would have been incarcerated, at least overnight. But after taking me to the station for an interview, they took me home. They were very good to me. There were two uniformed officers and one plainclothes. They were very professional. I lied through my teeth in the first interview. I was very scared. I think I did a pretty good job of hiding it, but I was scared.

When I went back the second time to confess, it was a huge relief. I felt much, much better about the situation. I finally felt I had done the right thing after a long, long time.

D. What led you to turn yourself in and confess?

M. I realized that this was not going to play out well. That it was going to totally divide the family and betray them more than I already had. By me denying everything, it was more abuse on Linda. To drag her through a trial was unthinkable. I most likely could have won, if I had played it totally cool and calculated and denied, denied, denied. If I had totally lawyered up and done everything they had told me to do, I could probably have beat it—but there would have been a big mess in the family and I just really.... I knew I was going away for a long time and I wasn't coming back. I wasn't going to incur any lawyers fees for my family. I was just going to plead guilty to everything. I didn't care if I went away for life. I knew the best thing for me to do was admit it. Take the lumps. That was my intent.

D. In case someone who is fantasizing about molesting a child reads this interview, I'd like them to understand the price they'll pay. Could you tell me exactly what happened from the time you turned yourself in?

M. After making my statement, I was put into a holding cell by myself at the O.P.P. station. I was so relieved to finally have the truth out. There was a nice old lady working there and so I started to talk to her and told her how good I felt to have done the right thing. She stood there and asked me what the charges were and I told her. She just went white and became very belligerent and got right on the phone. The constable who I had been talking with came up to my cell and said, "I'm only going to tell you this once. When you go over to the jail, keep your mouth *shut*. People do not want to know about this charge, and so for your own self-preservation, ... and it was very good advice.

But then, when they took me over to the jail, the guards over there already knew. And so all of this stuff started to happen.

D. That lady told them?

M. I don't know. The guards who carry you over have a record of what you're charged with so that they can process you in. So it started with the strip-search with the guards berating me and marching me naked, carrying my jail clothes, in front of everybody in the holding cells with them all yelling at me about how they were going to get me.... I really... I really don't want to go there.

D. Remember, the reason why I'm asking you about the details of this is in hopes that it will be a deterrent to anyone else who is thinking about molesting a child and so that victims will feel that they have had some justice.

M. Yeah. It's hell on earth. You can't believe how alone you are. I basically went nuts for a little while. They psychologically broke me. I was totally delusional for a couple of days at least.

D. What did they do to break you?

M. No sleep. They put me in a padded blanket-garment sort of dress thing with straps made from safety belt fabric over my shoulders. I was strapped into it. I had no clothes. They had taken everything I had. They control the temperature in the cells and so they turned my heat right down so that it was a very cold cell. All I had was a tiny little blanket about two feet by four feet, made of the same fabric as this dress thing. It was basically what they call their "suicide watch." There was one guard watching me. I don't know his name, but I'll never forget his face. He was a guy who was big in the union and very belligerent. It was that guy who made the decision that I was going to go into the cold cell. I was taken to a nurse and of the corner of my eye I caught him give her a big wink that this was going to happen.

So they kept me there for three days. Basically, they would stay outside my door and taunt me and tell me how terrible I was. They'd carry on conversations outside my door about all the horrible things they'd heard I did. If I did go to sleep at all, they'd bang on my door to make me wake up. So I'd had no sleep at all and was very, very cold for three days.

Then at five in the morning, they took me down to a holding cell to wait until 8:30 to be loaded into a paddy wagon to go to the courthouse. So I was just left there to wait in this absolutely filthy cell. I think they must smear these places with excrement on purpose so that they are as miserable as they can possibly be. The walls are just covered with feces.

D. You mean in the cells below the courthouse?

M. No—in the Super Jail, but the courtroom cells are the same. There are some cells that are okay, and then there are others that are just terrible. When I was first going through all that, I was always put in the worst ones for obvious reasons. It's like a game to some of these people. The worst guards were the women, by far, but in general, there a lot of very, very good people there.

D. Earlier, you spoke of the "perp walk." What was that?

M. After they strip search you, they're supposed to give you an orange jumpsuit with underwear and slippers and you should be able to put those on, because there are five or six low-walled cement cubicles so that when you return from court, you're supposed to strip out of your street clothes back into the prison wear in those cubicles. But instead of that, when a prisoner like me is taken from the holding cell to the regular cells, they make them stay naked, just carrying their prison clothes and walk past all these holding cells, some of which can hold as many as 30 men. Some hold ten or twenty and then there are some cells with just one man. They let these guys know what the charges are and so as I walked down the hall, all these guys were yelling profanities and threats about how they were going to get me. It was.... So that was the perp walk.

D. So that happened when you first got there?

M. I turned myself in on Saturday morning and spent Saturday night in a holding cell in the O.P.P. Station. Sunday morning, I did video court from there. Then I was transported to the Super Jail Sunday afternoon and that's where the perp walk and everything else started. That's when I was taken up to the psyche ward and put in the cold cell for three days, supposedly on suicide watch. But every time I was taken back and forth to court, it was like a perp walk because the other prisoners were made aware of what the charges were.

D. Did you ever find yourself in grave danger?

M. Yes. Many times. There were times when I could have been killed—people who wanted to kill me. But God was there and protected me the whole time.

D. You've talked about being active in a church. How could you call yourself a Christian?

M. I had committed my life to God and believed everything in the

Bible. I just wasn't following what it said. I put my own desires ahead of everything and didn't work at applying Scripture to my life. I was just a guy sitting in a pew saying all the right things but doing whatever I felt like doing.

Did you feel as though God had left you in prison?

M. No, although I certainly deserved to have Him leave me. There were so many occurrences when really bad things could have happened. I could have died. Just on my pod there were several guys who would have killed me as quick as they would have looked at me if they could have gotten their hands on me. I feel that God gave me wisdom in what to say, what to do and how to react. Whenever I would ask Him what I was to do in a particular situation, I would just feel a flood of peace and I knew He was with me. I'd do whatever it was I felt He told me to do and I was protected.

D. After all of that, do you still have an attraction to children?

M. No. Quite frankly, I've gone overboard the other way. I'm frightened of children now. If I'm in a grocery store and there are a couple of kids in an aisle without their mother, I'll turn my cart around and go the opposite direction. It's just common good sense. It's not that I'm afraid of re-offending, because that's not going to happen. My fear is that I'll be perceived as doing something inappropriate. I'm extremely careful not to put myself in a position where anyone could get the wrong idea.

D. How do you feel about yourself now, generally?

M. I'm just a work in progress. I have difficulty with some things. For instance, in my work, I can't get overly friendly with anybody or invite them to church because if they come to my church, I'll lose my job. Someone there will ask if they know about my background—and that will be it. I'll be history. Any effect I have on people just has to be through the way I live my life, through being a person who is not profane, who is honest and helpful—but I can't invite them to come to my church. And that's just the facts of life. That understanding comes through the first job I got after I was released at a trucking company. I was the best night watchman they had ever had—until one guy found out that I had been in prison and that was it. So it makes that part of it difficult.

D. How do you feel about yourself now in relation to other people?

M. I feel as though I'll always be in a fishbowl. Everybody is reading behind the lines, wondering what I'm doing. I know my pastor and his church board are pleased that I'm doing everything to earn their respect and keep people comfortable and stick to the reintegration plan without being reminded. For instance, I'd never go to the washroom in the church. If I had to go, I'd leave the building and go home and go there. It's just staying away from any perception of acting questionably.

It's difficult because I can't just go out anywhere and socialize and tell anybody about my past and expect anyone to be supportive, because it's just not going to happen. So I'm isolated. I can't just go out and be a normal person. I'm just coming to grips with that now and realizing that that's always the way life is going to be for me. It's my fault – nobody else's.

I do feel very good about my relationship with my parole officer and my psychologist. They are very positive about the support group I have. The fact that my sister and my aunt have been so incredibly supportive says a lot to them and has meant so much to my ability to rebuild my life.

Most of the guys like me don't have the support group I have. They've lost everybody and they just give up. They basically re-offend so that they can go back in to get off the streets. They're with out any means and life is just too terrible on the outside.

D. Are you still a manipulator?

M. I don't think so. I hope not. I try to be totally frank and honest about everything and I think that is the key. If someone asks me a direct question, I'm not going to lie about it. For instance, if some one asks me at my work if I have been in prison for child molestation, I'm not about to lie about it. I'll say yes and then I might as well go out and get in my car because I'm going to lose my job. So from that standpoint, I'm not that same person anymore.

I think that's why a few of my old friends and my sister and aunt have stuck by me, because there's been a trust factor built up which I very much cherish. Without it I'd be totally lost. I'd be totally out of my mind, I guess. That's all I can do.

Now, I recognize my lot in life. If I didn't have the backing of my support group, I know I'd be in big trouble. I think I'd just collapse. But I do think that God has brought this support group together. It just seems supernatural to me. I was never that close to my aunt or my sister until this happened.

D. What role does remorse play in your life? How do you deal with the shame?

M. I don't call it remorse. That may sound strange. I call it reality. There are realities that I have to live with for the rest of my life. There is an awareness of how deeply this has adversely affected the people in my life. Their woes right now are caused primarily by me and I'm aware of that.

Remorse and shame? This has taught me to see the girls as real people with emotions, thoughts and needs. I betrayed their trust and I feel very badly because I took advantage of their vulnerability.

D. What will you do if the temptation returns?

M. I'm going at life in such a way as to not allow the temptation to return. I've purposed myself to walk away from any possibly compromising situations.

I read a lot and keep myself busy with work and church. When impure thoughts come into my mind, I replace them with positive, healthy thoughts or good memories. The key is not ignoring bad thoughts—it's replacing them. I know that I can talk to my pastor about anything, anytime. We have both come to the conclusion that man, left to his own desires, is very dark. We are all tempted, but left to run rampant, the imagination can be a disastrous thing.

D. So you'd say it's all about renewing the mind?

M. Knowing exactly what the pitfalls are and how to avoid them is critical. Replacing dark thoughts. That's why Philippians, Chapter Four, is so important to me. *"Whatever is true, whatever is noble, whatever is right, whatever is pure, whatever is lovely, whatever is admirable—if anything is excellent or praiseworthy—think about such things."* If a temptation comes into my mind, I immediately capture that thought and replace it with something else. Often a memory, like laying on my back, looking up at the stars with one of my grandchildren... that was such a wonderful, solid memory. Or driving down to the lake with my old dog, Jack. The point is that you can't *not* think about something, or it becomes the elephant in the room. It becomes bigger and more important. You have to replace it with something positive. Something better.

D. If you could say anything to your victims, what would it be?

M. That I'm very sorry. I know that sounds like a very trite thing to say. I wish there had been an opportunity for them to confront me – for everyone who this touched to confront me and be able to express how I hurt them. I know that the victim impact statements are meant to do that, but the girls weren't there when I read them. I would like them to know how sorry I truly am. I don't deserve forgiveness, but in the long haul, it is the only thing that will bring peace to them.

D. Is doing this interview an effort on your part to make some restitution?

The best thing I can do for my victims is to never offend again. As the perpetrator, nothing I say means a hill of beans. It's only what I do with the rest of my life that could make some small possible bit of difference to them. I'm aware of that. It may never make any difference and that thought makes me very sad, but it's a valid thought. It's a reality.

D. Is there anything I haven't asked?

M. There are no excuses for anyone to molest a child. No reasons. Every individual is responsible for his or her own choices. Mine were detestably self-gratifying. The road to healing starts with taking responsibility for your own actions. All of the repercussions I face were brought on by my own hand. They are no one else's fault.

Why do they do it???

My interview with Matt left me shaking my head. Why, for goodness sake, would a fully grown, married man want to manipulate a child into sexual interaction? It makes no sense.

Even if we figure it out with a gazillion studies, it doesn't erase the gut-wrenching consequences of their actions.

However, perhaps by trying to understand, some child, somewhere, will be protected.

While healthy humans are born with the propensity to engage in sexual activity, they're not born to be pedophiles or child molesters. Those desires are developed as a result of early experiences or interruptions in normal development.

Everyone needs to be touched and loved and paid attention to. As individuals mature, sexual satisfaction is added to the list of needs. During puberty, boys suddenly become totally preoccupied with sex. Their sex hormones increase five-fold within a two year period. Whatever sexual messages are delivered to them during that period are naturally going to have great significance. If they have normal interactions with females during that time, they are more likely to develop as heterosexuals. On the other hand, if they are socially awkward and experience sexual arousal with the same sex or with someone considerably younger, it will be remembered as pleasurable and they may begin to seek out that source of arousal again and again, rather than changing the brain cues and seeking satisfaction from the normal, healthy source.

Of course the motivations are different with each person and they change over time. They are as varied as individual childhoods and early experiences. A rapist or a sadist, for example, is going to differ in motivations from a man who touches the genitals of a single child.

Sometimes, the motivation has nothing to do with sex. For a sadistic rapist, it may be all about hostility and cruelty. For a gentle molester, it may be all about control or power imbalance, perhaps as a reinforcement of his "ownership" of the child. Or it could be enjoyment of the respect for authority he gets from children, but seldom from his peers.

Jocelyn, the sad-eyed, once-pretty mother of three sons, sat with me one rainy afternoon and recounted her heart breaking experience. With too many lines etched in her face, she told me about her precious middle son who had been molested by a close family friend.

> My son's molester claimed that his father molested him, so it felt natural. He said he was just "teaching (my son) about sex." When I heard those words, I was enraged - *enraged!* How *dare* he rob my son of the carefree innocence of childhood! How *dare* he rob me of my parental privilege and responsibility before my son was old enough to know about such things! How *dare* he masquerade helpfulness for selfishness! How *dare* he impose himself on my son as the first experience with sex! How *dare* he dupe me into believing that his home was the safest place in the world for my little boy to be? How *dare* he express his darkest, most vile imaginings on my sweet child? How *dare* he carry on a relationship with my family for years, hiding this terrible secret? How *dare* he subject my son to the lifelong challenges of a molested child? How *dare* he pretend to be such a fine, upstanding, charming member of society?

She paused and then continued.

> I never thought I would be able to smile again. My child's molester seemed to think it was just fine to use whoever was accessible to involve in his sex life. And yet he *knew* it was wrong because he kept it hidden. He seemed to have no concept of respect for boundaries.

A study by Briggs and Hawkins[27] found that sex abusers who were abused themselves as children often regarded their own abuse as "normal," sometimes even enjoyable. In contrast, the non-offenders they studied who had also been abused as children, were more likely to report their own abuse as negative. Thus the study speculated that men who normalized their own experience of sexual abuse may be more likely to become abusers themselves and then fail to understand the harm they have caused.

Whatever the reasons for the criminal behavior, we can only try to get a handle on the "why," so that if we catch a glimpse of someone developing this kind of mind set, we can try to divert their course for the protection of some unknown child sometime, somewhere.

Dr Jeckyll – Mr. Hyde

A pedophile can be an unshaven stranger who hangs around playgrounds, obviously scoping out his prey; or perhaps the executive on the 34th floor, or maybe a neighbour like Matt – or – the stranger can be a husband with whom one has lived for 38 years.

Some data suggest that up to one-third of child molesters are female.[28] Accurate statistics are impossible to compile because abuse by women is often not reported and often not considered abuse. While contradictory studies show that number to be much smaller, we do know that the majority are men.

27. Briggs, F., & Hawkins, R.M.F. (1996). A comparison of the childhood experiences of convicted male child molesters and men who were sexually abused in childhood and claimed to be non offenders. Child Abuse and Neglect, 20, 221-33.
28. Van Dam, Carla (2001). *Identifying Child Molesters, Preventing Child Sexual Abuse by Recognizing the Patterns of the Offenders*, New York: The Halworth Maltreatment and Trauma Press, p.56.

Despite child advocate John Walsh's advice to parents never to hire a male baby sitter, however, it's important not to marginalize men. Some go so far as to say that people who refuse to hire male nannies (mannies) are practising male profiling, not unlike police who pull drivers over for DWH: "Driving While Hispanic or Hungarian." While it's important to foster warm relationships between wonderful, healthy men and children, a refusal to hire a male baby sitter is not about equal rights or profiling. It's just about minimizing risk. Having said that, for the sake of simplicity, most references are to "he" in this book.

A child molester can be a doctor, a garbage-collector, a teacher, a musician, a son, a brother, a teenager, a senior, a billionaire, a pauper, a homosexual, a heterosexual, a Christian, a Buddhist or an agnostic. He can be fighting trim or flabby; American, French, Russian or Oriental. He can be the recognized ex-convict down the street who has served his time—or he can be the nice man next door whose worst known offence was a speeding ticket in 1997. He can be the gentle grandpa or the personable baby-sitter.

It used to be that parents warned their little ones not to talk to strangers. However, today's research relegates stranger danger to a smaller role. Tragically, the greatest incidence of child sexual abuse is within the family. In L. Halliday's research[29] on over 1,000 subjects, only 13 percent of the abuse was committed by strangers. Fifty-seven percent was committed by family members and 28 percent involved friends. Twenty-one percent involved natural fathers, 12 percent stepfathers, 10 percent

29. Halliday, L. (1985). Sexual Abuse: Counseling issues and concerns. Campbell River, B.C., Ptarmigan Press.

uncles, 10 percent brothers, five percent grandfathers, 19 percent family friends and three percent baby-sitters. Children in step-families are at greater risk because, with the addition of more extended family, more people have easy access to them.While numbers differ according to the differing studies, it's impossible to document exact numbers or demographics because so many incidents go unreported.

One thing is clear: the stereotype of the "dirty old man" is misleading. There's general agreement that the majority of offenders are under the age of 35.[30]

In a 1986 interview in *The New York Times*, Ted Bundy, one of America's worst killers, a handsome, articulate law student working in the Republican party, said, "What people have to realize is that...in all significant respects, I am essentially like everybody else." His lawyer, James Coleman said, "He's your next-door neighbor. People don't want to believe that their next-door neighbor can behave like this."

Unless convicted, pedophiles and child-molesters don't come with labels that warn people. If convicted, the labels mean little because it's impossible to know whether the bearers will ever offend again. It is possible that the least dangerous man is the one who has been caught, served his time and truly dealt with his dark heart. It is possible that the most dangerous person is the unsuspected man who sits beside one in church.

---

30. Abel, G., Becker, J., Mittleman, M., Rouleau, J., and Murphy, W. (1987). Journal of Interpersonal Violence, 2(1), March, p.3-25.

Child molester or pedophile?

It can be helpful to know that child molesters are not necessarily pedophiles and pedophiles are not necessarily child molesters. Pedophilia is a psychological disorder defined by a distinct sexual preference for pre-pubescent children. The Diagnostic and Statistical Manual of Mental Disorders (DSM 111-R), published by the American Psychological Association, gives the following definition of pedophilia:

> "Recurrent, intense, sexual urges and sexual arousing fantasies of at least six months duration involving sexual activity with a pre-pubescent child."[31]

Thus, an individual can be a pedophile without actually engaging in a sexual act. Simply having fantasies about sexual activity with a child over a period of at least six months will qualify. Many pedophiles never engage in actual criminal activity. They just stay at home and think about it. They often have large collections of child pornography or child erotica. Staying close to children is high on their list of priorities. The most common type of pedophile is the immature individual who has never been very successful maintaining peer relationships. Those who lack social contact often spiral down deeper and deeper into a fantasy world.

Pedophiles who actually engage in child molestation become "child molesters." They often use their collections of erotica and pornography to show to their victims as part of the grooming process of seduction. They think that when their victims see the photographs, their inhibitions will be lowered and they'll be

31. Diagnostic and Statistical Manual of Mental Disorders (DSM 111-R), The American Psychological Association, 1987.

more inclined to accept sexual activity as something people do normally. Some use photographs and videos they have made of their victims to blackmail them into further sexual activity.

Child molesters, on the other hand, by definition engage in sexual acts with children, but they will generally go after older victims as well as children. Ninety-five percent of them are male. Only 10 percent are strangers to their victims. Fifty to 60 percent are family members. According to a Public Health Agency of Canada fact sheet, 25 percent of molesters are teenagers. The rule of thumb used by professionals is that child sexual abuse occurs when a person touches a child for sexual gratification and is four years older than the child. (Curious playmates of the same age are protected by the age issue.)

Because family members are often hidden from the criminal justice system, it's difficult for researchers to get a handle on the true extent of the problem. They have been more successful in characterizing family friends and trusted adults outside of the family. These people usually don't use violence on their victims. Like Matt, they "groom" them, or set them up for the molestation by gradually establishing bonds with the child. By the time the first touch happens, the child has been so conditioned that he or she hardly knows what's happening.

Molesters victimize children for other motives as well as sexual gratification. Sometimes it's just part of the mistreatment they direct toward people in general. Usually, they have low self-esteem and view children as less powerful objects on which to vent their anger or sexual frustrations. The main criteria for choosing a victim is availability. It could be anyone, anywhere, who happens to be in the wrong place at the wrong time. They can be strangers who forcefully attack children they don't know or individuals or family known to the child who use the situation to their own advantage with no concern for the victim.

Those child molesters who prefer sex with children can have an astounding number of victims over a lifetime, if not caught. They choose particular victims and groom them for abuse through developing a relationship of trust, buying them gifts and honing in on their emotional weaknesses. According to U.S. Department of Justice statistics, in more than 90 percent of cases of child rape, the offender was well-known to the children or their parents. These are pedophiles who have carried their fantasies into reality. Some are brutal and physically cruel, while others are more gentle in their approaches. They manipulate relationships to the point of expressing their perversions.

The newest twist to the oldest perversion

In 1874, the police in London, England, arrested a photographer with 130,000 pornographic images of children.[32] In those days, the images were on glass plates. Child pornography is nothing new. Stories of incest filter way back in biblical times to the story of Lot and his daughters.

What is new is that pedophiles are becoming increasingly empowered through the use of the Internet. They used to be a solitary lot, isolated by the shame of their perversions and repressed by the revulsion of normal society.

But now! Now they can go online and, with a click of the mouse, find like-minded people with whom to share not only photographs, but actual live occurrences of child rape and molestation. While Chapter Five, "The Porn Factor," addresses this more fully, the point here is that pedophiles are no longer

32. Sher, Julian, *One Child at a Time*, Random House Canada, p.36.

the isolated loners they once were. Thanks to the Internet, they are part of a slimy club of peers they can access at any moment, day or night, and feed their perversions. Because of the group solidarity, they feel more legitimized and thus are becoming bolder and bolder. Because of the group dynamic, they are interacting more like a repressed minority than an intolerable plague.

Victims as child molesters

While a study by Briggs and Hawkins revealed that more than 93 percent of convicted child molesters suffered abuse as children[33], being a victim of sexual abuse does not naturally lead to being an offender as an adult. There are far too many victims for that to be the case. It is estimated that up to 48 million women and up to 22 million men in the United States have suffered molestation before the age of 18. Also, the fact that more than twice as many women as men are victimized, while most of the molesters are men, does not gel with the theory of the victim necessarily becoming a victimizer.

Sadly, many molesters or potential molesters never disclose the abuse they themselves have received, thus short-circuiting any possibility of treatment prior to acting out their own fantasies. I believe that part of the purpose of marriage is to help each other heal from the wounds of childhood. Thoughts of "if only I had..." are sad refrains sung by unsuspecting families of eventually convicted molesters who wish they had been given the opportunity to help him to heal. In many cases, if that had happened, precious children would not have had to suffer...

33. Briggs, F., & Hawkins, R.M.F. (1996). A comparison of the childhood experiences of convicted male child molesters and men who were sexually abused in childhood and claimed to be non offenders. Child Abuse and Neglect, 20, 221-33.

Recognize the Warning Signs

While it is often a total shock to those who know him when a pedophile or a child molester is revealed, there are sometimes signs that no one wants to recognize until they are no longer possible to ignore.

For instance, Janice (name changed), the wife of a convicted molester, told me that it always bothered her that whenever they went to visit friends, her husband would seem to want to spend more time with the children than with the adults. In her words:

> It was embarrassing, because I felt he was sending a message to our hosts that they weren't interesting enough for him. He thought nothing of leaving a room of adults to spend time with children, sometimes in their rooms. To me, it was highly inappropriate to go anywhere in someone else's house without an adult leading the way—but normally accepted social boundaries didn't seem to faze him. If I were to complain on the way home, he would deny having spent an inappropriately greater amount of time with the children than with the adults, making me feel like a prissy complainer. Because there was no actual evidence of him doing anything to a child, I simply felt uncomfortable and confused about his behavior. Eventually, it became easier to stay home than to socialize and have to risk offending our friends or have them wonder about my husband, to say nothing of going home in an argument.

Kia, another wife of a convicted molester said,

> It bothered me that whenever young girls would visit my grandchildren, Joseph would seem more interested in them than I felt was normal. I chalked it up to him being emotionally immature, the result of some unknown influence that had kept him trapped in adolescence. Whenever young female friends needed transportation or help of any kind, he was right there,

> offering to help before having to be asked. With my busy life, I appreciated his helpfulness enormously. The children always seemed to love his attentions and it made me feel like a spoil-sport if I were to complain. I remembered all of my wonderful uncles who had given me such a lovely sense of importance in this world and tried to reassure myself that Joseph was doing the same for these children.

Many mothers and grandmothers might think such a willing spirit was too good to be true. For these women, it was.

Kia went on to say,

> One of the young girls who was a frequent visitor in our home came from a very dysfunctional family. Lacking the stability and attention she needed, she responded wholeheartedly to Joseph's attentions and was forever wanting to sit on his knee, comb his hair and generally be with him wherever he went. If I were to try to deter her or voice any discomfort about it, Joseph would remind me that she needed a sense of security and the knowledge that she was special to people.
>
> Looking back, it's more than obvious to me that I was naîve. But at the time, I didn't dream Joseph would actually *do* anything inappropriate. My fear was that someone might incorrectly suspect his motives because it wasn't normal behavior—it was never that he would ever actually molest a child! In my heart of hearts, I believed him to be foolishly opening himself up for suspicion—*never dreaming* that any suspicion would be grounded. He angered me with his stupidity. I felt that I had to protect him from people who might not understand how harmless, helpful and loving he was. I thought he was just a big, gentle teddy bear.

In retrospect, sadly, painfully, the warning signs were clear.

Who is the Predator?

Dr. Charles Whitfield found that the most effective cover a child molester has is the *desire* of people not to know. When offenders deny their guilt, people want so much to believe that it didn't happen that it resonates with their own personal hopes and beliefs about the incident.

Manipulative molesters play on the doubts of normal people that someone who appears respectable would ever do such a horrible thing. Because people don't want to believe it, if someone they care about is charged with a sexual crime, they try desperately to find some other logical explanation for the child's disclosure. Because the majority of people are not suspicious and generally trust others, particularly if they are attractive and polite, they enable child molesters to harm children.

In the course of researching her book, *Identifying Child Molesters*,[34] Dr. Carla van Dam interviewed over 300 molesters who exhibited similar types of behaviors in social situations. While there is no precise profile to identify predators, these similar behaviors provide us with a general pattern to watch for. If an individual exhibits enough of these behaviors to arouse concern, he needs to be considered too risky to be allowed unsupervised around our children.

No predator will exhibit all of the signs common to molesters, simply because of human individuality. However, he or she will generally exhibit a combination of the signs in the following list:

- There will be a general feeling of discomfort in the presence of the person in question.

34. Van Dam, Carla (2001). *Identifying Child Molesters, Preventing Child Sexual Abuse by Recognizing the Patterns of the Offenders,* New York: The Halworth Maltreatment and Trauma Press.

- An emotionally dysfunctional adult may pay particular attention to a needy child.
- He may show a preference for association with children.
- The person in question maintains few friendships in his own age bracket.
- He has structured access to children. In order to groom a child and his or her parents for the abuse, a child molester has to have a legitimate connection to the child that will allow for the process of time the "grooming" takes. Teaching, bus driving, sports coaching, camp counseling and volunteering to help with children's activities, all offer opportunities to be alone with children with no parental supervision.
- He encourages a child to develop feelings, entrapping the young victim in a situation where the child feels that the abuse is legitimized by his or her feelings for the abuser. This is a psychological process known as the "Stockholm Syndrome" where victims develop feelings of attachment to their captors. (As the victims mature, the affection for the abuser usually dwindles and the painful truth emerges.)
- The person in question may have frequent changes of residence or jobs without much discussion about the reasons for the changes.
- While pedophiles most often have failed marriages because of their sexual preference, they often stay in the marriage to mask their true intentions. The mate becomes a "front" for a respectable life. While they may indicate to the wife that they simply have no interest in sex, the reality may be quite the opposite.

- There may be a continuation of inappropriate association with children despite concerns expressed by others.
- They may appear disconnected from normal peers.
- They may make reference to children in particularly exalted terms, such as "beautiful," "adorable," or other labels that are said in a way that seem excessive.
- They may seem to have disrespect for social boundaries.
- They may exhibit behavior that seems too good to be true, perhaps being overly helpful.
- They may have a desire for hobbies that seem more appropriate for a child than for an adult, like building miniature trains, collecting toys or whatever.
- They may have either a particularly charming personality or obvious 'loner' qualities, sometimes a combination of both. The charmers are socially appealing but often lack substance in their relationships. There's no sense of genuine bonding at a heart level.
- Lack of development of the capacity for intimacy, resulting in emotional loneliness.
- There may be interaction with young teens at a peer level, engaging in conversations about sex, crushes or whatever would not be normally of interest for an adult to discuss with a teen.
- Playing with children at a peer level; tickling, play fighting

etc., to gain confidence and rapport and introduce the child to touching. As the child becomes desensitized to touch in appropriate places, the touch progresses to breasts and genitals.

- Response to concerns with denial and aggression, making the concerned individual feel like a fool
- Maintenance of an image of social acceptability, often taking leadership in children's groups through which to gain the trust of parents and children alike.

Any of these warning signs need to be viewed within the context of an individual's life. For instance, if someone enjoys playing with children *in the company of other adults*, that's normal. If someone is a particularly helpful person but *doesn't seek out the company of children*, that's a wonderful thing. However, if combinations of the above qualities are evident, there's cause for concern and children need to be carefully watched around these people.

The alarming revelations of hundreds of men in the 1990s and 2000s of childhood sexual molestation by Catholic priests are sad testimony to the compulsions of some predators who live their whole lives victimizing children until the day they are caught. Some have a history of using hundreds of children over their lifetimes. Such revelations have been shattering, but in Chapter Four, "Predators in Pews and Pulpits," it will become evident that one denomination is no purer than any other with regard to abuse.

The manipulative molester

One characteristic shared by all child molesters is that they are finely tuned manipulators and they recognize their adeptness at manipulating people to achieve their own ends.

In her book, *The Manipulative Man*, Dorothy McCoy referred to the ICD-10 (the mental health manual used in Europe) in listing the following characteristics[35] to watch for in classifying someone as a manipulator:

- Callous unconcern for the feelings of others
- Gross and persistent attitude of irresponsibility and disregard for social norms, rules and obligations
- Incapacity to maintain enduring relationships, though having no difficulty in establishing them
- Very low tolerance to frustration and a low threshold for discharge of aggression, including violence
- Incapacity to experience guilt or to profit from experience, particularly punishment
- Marked proneness to blame others, or to offer plausible rationalizations, for the behavior that has brought the patient into conflict with society.

While these are guidelines for identification, not every manipulator will exhibit all of the characteristics and those who do, will do so in greater and lesser degrees.

Manipulative men hide in plain sight. They hide their true selves from everyone. Whenever Kia tried to connect with her husband on a deep heart level, he would shrug his shoulders and say, "I'm not a very deep guy. This is all there is."

Although most manipulators are aware of rules and taboos,

35. McCoy, D. (2006). *The Manipulative Man*, Adams Media, Avon, Mass. p.9.

they have no respect for them. The fact that they are so crafty in hiding their deeds demonstrates that they know very well that what they are doing is wrong.

The "moment"

Whether or not a perpetrator is discovered and incarcerated, there is a "moment" when they have to admit that the consequences of their choices are so bad that life is out of control for them.

For a public figure, this may be the news making moment when flashbulbs are popping as the police escort him from his house to a waiting cruiser.

For a father, it may be the moment his son finds his stash of pornography.

For a priest, minister or rabbi, it could be the first moment alone as he lies on his hard cell mattress.

Who is the Predator?

Who is the Predator? Only she or he knows – until the silence is broken.

We are called the "guardians" of our children because we must always stand on guard for them, daring to face the reality that those we may know and love are not beyond falling prey to the darkest inclinations of their hearts.

Do we have to live in fear and paranoia? No. We can live in a spirit of love for our fellow man, the knowledge that we, as parents, grandparents and community, are empowered through diligence to protect our children, and that with soundness of mind, we can overcome the fallout from darkness.

Predator-Proofing our Children

Incredibly, we entrust the identification of pedophiles to the smallest, most vulnerable members of society—our children! We think that by teaching them about "good touch/bad touch," how to say "no" and to tell us if anyone crosses the line, we can train them to be responsible for their own protection. Then we relax, thinking our kids have been prepared and empowered and we've done our jobs.

But we have lulled ourselves to sleep! It's not enough! I did that with my children and still one of them was victimized over a long period of time, not knowing how to tell.

There is no proof that "bad touch" warnings prevent child sexual abuse. Available data shows that few children are able to learn to apply this training before the third grade. I was unable to find any studies that showed that children who are trained are any more successful at warding off attackers than untrained children. Most victims have been given these warnings by loving parents, yet have fallen prey. Unfortunately, the training has brought confusion into non-abuse situations like healthy tickling and bathing and heightened the anxiety levels of children.[36]

36. D, Finkelhor and J. Dziuba-Leatherman, (1995). Victimization prevention programs: A national survey of children's exposure and reactions, Child Abuse & Neglect, 19: 129-39.

The reality is that some offenders are more effective in their threats or methods of intimidation or instilling guilt than others. From a chld's perspective, it can seem impossible to resist or to tell what has happened. For instance, being told that your whole family will be killed if you dare to tell is way too big a risk to take; or imagine sitting on a beloved grandpa's knee, being told that if you say anything about him touching you in the wrong place, he will be taken to jail and it will be your fault for telling on him.

On top of failing to prevent the actual victimization, we can unthinkingly impose guilt upon our children for failing to alert anyone to what is happening. They can feel that they are at fault for the assault.

Another problem with counting on children to identify molesters, is the reality that in order for a child to identify a potential molester, he or she has to be subjected to an approach, if not an actual victimization. The hope of this book is that many children will be protected before they find themselves face to face with a molester.

Teaching the importance of being trustworthy

Then there's the problem of trusting children who don't necessarily always tell the truth. How do they feel if they do exactly as we've told them to do—and then we don't believe them when they really need us to believe because they've told lies in the past?

My research was not limited to libraries or news reports. I gained valuable insight from individuals who were willing to expose their hearts in interviews in hopes that their sharing would assist in the battle to protect children.

One of these contributors was Sondra, a grandmother who found herself caught between her husband, who she thought was truthful, and his victim, who she knew had not always been trustworthy. Sondra says:

> Today, when I look back at all that happened under my radar, I weep. I was living my life totally devoid of reality, totally unaware of the dynamics and activities in my own home. If only—if only I had recognized the signs. Now, because I didn't believe my granddaughter when she revealed the truth, I don't have the privilege of a relationship with her. I was the adult. She was the child. In her heart, she was no doubt crying out for me to see beneath the secret she had to keep. I was supposed to be able to protect her. Not only did I not protect her from my husband—I didn't believe her in the traumatic moment of revelation. She and her father, my son, had to endure five days of me trying to figure out why she would tell such a terrible lie. When my husband finally confessed and I asked my granddaughter to forgive me for not believing her, it was too late. I don't know whether she or my son will ever really forgive me. Now, almost two years after her disclosure, she and I are still estranged and it breaks my heart. She is now sixteen years old. Sweet, precious sixteen.

Children in today's society can find themselves in a multiplicity of circumstances where manipulative adults tell them not to tell this or that, particularly in situations of abuse and custody battles. When adults teach children to be deceptive, there's no wonder that truth is often in short supply.

Children must be taught, encouraged, coached, mentored in truth telling. It is critical, not only so that we can believe them, but so that they will know they will be believed because of their history of trustworthiness.

Any adult who lies to a child, or allows a child to discover them in a lie, thus teaching them to lie by example, will have much for which to answer.

Obviously, we have to kick it up a notch and identify people who may harm our children before they get a chance to try. We have to take the responsibility of being our children's protectors.

We're living in a different world

Child molestation is nothing new. It's been around since the dawn of time, rotting the fabric of society. Until recently it has been discussed only in whispers, but in the past 10 years, newspapers have become more and more filled with stories of the sexual assault of children.

Pedophiles used to live like solitary moles, furtively looking at obscene photos of children in the dark corners of their lives. They had no one to talk to about their interests because they were too shameful.

Suddenly, the advent of the Internet gave them a forum for discussion with other like minded predators. Where the soul destroying pictures were once so difficult to procure, millions of images of depravity suddenly became available with the click of a mouse.

There's strength in numbers. Reinforcement brought an increased boldness. Child molesters began trading images and videoing scenes of the sexual abuse of children, brainwashing themselves into thinking they were some kind of an oppressed minority group.

Michael Brière was the 36-year-old computer programmer who raped, murdered and dismembered beautiful 10-year-old Holly

Jones in Toronto in 2003. Holly had simply been walking home from a friend's house and innocently passed Briere's house on the way. Unbeknownst to anyone, he had been looking at child pornography on the Web and had begun to have fantasies about having sex with a child. After a couple of years of indulging in his "dark secret," he became consumed with the idea. "I really wanted to have sex with a child. And that was all consuming. I just came out of my place and she was just there." For the sake of 40 minutes of indulging his darkest fantasy, Brière lost his place in the world and Holly was lost to the world.

Sexual abuse of children is becoming epidemic in our society. Whatever the sources or motivations, children are being abused in alarming numbers. Things have to change. We have to find ways to keep children safe and clean up the moral air we breath.

Kicking it up a notch

We used to feel as though we were doing our jobs as parents by hiring a decent looking baby-sitter if we were going out, locking our doors at night and generally keeping an eye on the kids at playgrounds, theme parks and shopping malls.

It's not enough. We have to find ways to protect our children not only from strangers we've never met, but from strangers who may live in our own homes or strangers who we've counted among our friends for many years.

Protecting a child from a stranger who abducts a child for the purposes of a sex crime is generally a matter of logistics—doing everything we can to make sure that the child cannot be taken. This can be difficult without being physically with the child 24/7. However, diligence in making sure the child is not left vulnerable is worth every moment of effort.

Predator-Proofing our Children

Protecting a child from the manipulative predator, who is often known to the child or the parents, is sometimes much more complex, as it involves screening every association the child experiences. In Chapter Two, "Who is the Predator?" I compiled a checklist of characteristics that could warn of possible dangers. We have to go down this checklist with everyone we know and make informed choices about who we allow to spend time with our children. At this point in the history of our society, limiting opportunities for anyone to interfere with a child is critical.

Kicking it up a notch means:

- In planning for a family, planning to be hands-on parents with the children having primary priority until they are old enough to look after themselves
- Putting alarms in our children's and grandchildren's bedrooms at adult height
- Keeping *both* eyes on our kids when we take them out,
- Holding their hands until they are of a reasonable age (no matter how much they may protest)
- Teaching children to look for a mommy with kids or a grandma if they get lost in a mall, because caring women are a whole lot more plentiful than security guards.
- Staying home more with children until they get old enough to stay alone
- Screening potential caregivers for criminal offenses through local and federal law-enforcement agencies —not being afraid to request the person's birth date, social security number and a list of places where they have lived. You'll need them for proper screening

- Occasionally popping in on your baby-sitter unannounced
- Being meticulously on time whenever a child is expecting to be picked up from extracurricular activities or from wherever
- Establishing who is allowed in the house with a baby-sitter while you're away and following-up
- Reading in a lawn chair or gardening when your kids play outside—anything that puts you with them
- Spending time at the home of your children's friends before allowing them to visit there on their own
- Encouraging children to bring their friends home to your house instead of going to theirs—knowing their friends
- Planning entertainment that involves the children
- Becoming involved in your children's activities. Involved parents are a big "turn off" for pedophiles.
- Not advertising your child's name on a backpack or other personal item
- Reducing the desirability of your child by not dressing your child in alluring clothing
- Keeping in mind the fact that predators look for ease of approach and ease of retreat
- Making sure to choose a day-care or school with an "open door policy" that allows full visibility from the hallway at all times and making it clear that your child is not to be left with anyone but the primary caregiver without your knowledge
- Attending your child's lessons and other activities or sending someone you trust to accompany them

- Not allowing the internet in the privacy of a bedroom
- Taking the cameras off of computers
- Reinstating family discussions and family meals where open communication with the child is firmly established—also one-on-one open communication
- Supplying kids with emergency cell phones or GPS gadgets
- Supplying them with information such as what to do if they've been locked in a car trunk
- Teaching children that their bodies are their own and that it's okay to decline any touching or contact that makes them uncomfortable, particularly parts that are usually covered by a bathing suit or underwear, with the exception of bath time towelling dry with a parent or guardian and visits to the doctor with a nurse present
- Teaching children to tell about anyone who exposes themselves or shows them pictures of private parts
- Teaching children when it's okay to talk back to an adult—when they're told to do something that doesn't seem right to them
- Teaching children that if any adult asks them to keep a secret, no matter how bad it may be, they need to tell the parent immediately and they don't need to be afraid of consequences from the person who wanted them to keep the secret
- Taking parenting courses to give confidence in being in control of your child
- Never ignoring a child's protests about spending time with a certain adult—encouraging the child to tell you why and what is going on there

- Getting a grip on the reality that you are taking a grave risk if you send your child off on a *solitary* walk or bike ride. Any parent of a child who has been taken will say they would gladly have put their own interests aside to bike or walk with the child if they had the opportunity to do things over again. We are living in a different world than the one in which we were raised and we cannot pretend that the danger rate is the same.
- Paying special attention to friendships involving older persons, even older teens
- Helping kids going through puberty to manage their own sexual feelings
- Setting boundaries with girlfriends and boyfriends
- Handling peer pressure regarding pornography and violent or sexual video games
- Watching carefully for signs of abuse—physical and emotional—and not being afraid to question it directly

Besides the benefit of providing more safety for our children, this is the kind of stuff that makes for close families later on. It's hands-on caring. The other benefit is that it will make the child feel so much more secure.

Is it stifling? smothering? over-protective? paranoid? When balanced against loss or harm, those words all lose any meaning.

Whom Can We Trust?

No one should ever have to distrust the safety of a grandparent's home or the honor of a best friend around one's children—but that was the way it used to be, not the way it is today. Even after screening people, how do we know for sure who the molesters will be? Can we trust no one? Is everyone suspect? Do we have to live totally paranoid lives?

It's not about blanket distrust or paranoia. Just as we don't have to be paranoid to put life vests on our kids in the boat in case of an accident, we don't have to think we're being paranoid to eliminate situations where our children could be at risk.

It's about paying closer attention and listening to gut instincts that something may not be right. It's about forcing ourselves to pursue suspicion rather than turning a blind eye to odd behavior, even in those we may love. If we don't allow our minds to consider the horror of them being potential predators, we may miss the critical indicators.

Does this mean that if we have suspicions about Uncle Harold that we should deny him access to his nieces or nephews?

No. It simply means that, as parents or grandparents, we don't allow Johnny or Susie out of our sight at family reunions. No one has to know about our concerns. Running around like frazzled scatterbrains expressiong suspicion about everyone is totally counterproductive. It can actually work in the manipulator's advantage because it will result in more people telling you to calm down and potentially lead you to drop your guard in an effort to be more socially acceptable.

Does this mean that we have to report every suspicion to the police or that we have to prove that anyone exhibiting some or all of the warning signs is a predator?

No. It should be criminal to ruin a reputation without concrete evidence. We just have to step up to the plate and take responsibility for watching our children.

In most cases where a molester begins to "groom" a child (and the adults around the child) to allow him to make his move, if access to the child is removed, the danger will be eliminated. If your instincts sound the slightest alarm, simply remove the child. Don't allow yourself to be manipulated into allowing even a moment of unsupervised access again. Then, quietly keep an eye on the person in question for the protection of other children.

The "grooming" process

Once a pedophile sets his sights on a particular child, a process almost like "wooing" begins. However, it's not just about setting the child up to be victimized, it often involves the grooming of the parents as well.

These people are often well received by parents. They seem so nice—so accommodating—so helpful. What lovely people, we think. Some people *are* truly wonderful. The confusion lies in separating genuinely wonderful people from manipulative predators.

While it's critical to be aware of possible bad apples, it's also critical to maintain equilibrium, recognizing the fact that there are many fine people who gain trust with children and their families, who truly have the child's best interests at heart.

Dr. Anna Salter, Ph.D., who has worked with and written extensively about sex offenders, notes that, "a double life is prevalent among all types of sex offenders.... The front that offenders typically offer to the outside world is usually a 'good person,' someone who the community believes has a good character and would never do such a thing."[37]

37. Salter, Anna C. (2003). *Predators: Pedophiles, Rapists and Other Sex Offenders* , New York:

Dr. Salter found that child-molesters do whatever they can to allow themselves to have access to children while concealing their activities. This usually means finding responsible positions that allow them close proximity to children. They generally act very responsible socially and appear to be sincere, truthful people. Parents and others accept them at face value, believing the persona, thereby allowing the offender to have free and easy access to the child.

From material they compiled from predators, Elliott, Browne and Kilcoyne found that child sex offenders rarely choose their victims indiscriminately. They choose and set them up carefully. A child experiencing parental neglect is highly vulnerable. Pedophiles often pick children from broken families whose parents are distracted by their problems.

The way they operate is by seeking to exploit the emotional void in a lonely child's life by befriending them and showering them with gifts and attention. Bribery and games are commonly used, with the offender slowly desensitizing the child through touch, sex talk and persuasion.[38]

Dr. Salter reveals the careful planning a young pedophile put into grooming a victim:[39]

> "When a person like myself wants to obtain access to a child, you don't just go up and get the child and sexually molest the child. There's a process of obtaining the child's friendship and, in my case, also obtaining the family's friendship and their trust. When you get their trust, that's when the child becomes vulnerable and you can molest the child."

Basic Books, p.34.

38. Elliott, M., Browne, K., & Kilcoyne, J. (1995). Child Sexual Abuse Prevention: What Offenders Tell Us, Child Abuse & Neglect, 579-94.

39. Salter, Anna C. (2003). *Predators: Pedophiles, Rapists and Other Sex Offenders* , New York: Basic Books, p.42.

This is a clear demonstration of the gradual "grooming" process in which the predator manipulates the child into participating After establishing a friendship, the offender may start out by showing the child some pornography and telling him or her not to tell their parents. If the child keeps the secret, the offender may proceed to the next step, gradually escalating this kind of behavior until the child is desensitized enough to participate in more sexually progressed activity. The more secrets a child keeps, the more they may hesitate to disclose the abuse, possibly feeling responsible and ashamed of the sexual acts in which they were engaged.

The molester a child faces is not a statistic. He or she is a person—the outwardly caring teacher, the hockey coach or the seemingly kind relative who has worked hard to gain trust. The child is faced with either betraying that trust or keeping silent—a huge burden for a small child.

Managing the Internet

Pedophiles, pornographers and child molesters love the Internet. In protecting our children from this potential source of abuse, however, parents can do a great deal to eliminate risk.

Kids need to be made aware that if they respond to requests for photos of themselves, they could make themselves both the victims and creators of child pornography, running afoul of the law. With today's technology, there's no telling what could happen with a photo innocently sent for personal use, or what could be the actual motivations of the requester. It's no fun having a squad car drive up in one's driveway.

While we all want to trust our kids and have them believe that we trust them, the reality is that they are kids and immaturity leads people to do stupid things. According to the National Centre for Missing and Exploited Children, up to 10 percent of the material they seize has been produced by older children taking compromising photos of themselves on their webcams or cell phone cameras. They e-mail the pictures to themselves from their phones and then post them on the Web. Whether the motivation is teens acting out or a lonely girl persuaded to take photos of herself by someone she has "met" on the Internet, the risk is the same.

There's no real need to have a camera on a child's computer. Simply taking it off eliminates at least *one* area of risk.

Parents who complain about the effects of the Internet on their children, yet do nothing to supervise or control their children's access, have only themselves to blame. If they don't like it, yet have no means to control the negative influences on their children, they need to simply remove the Internet from the home. A computer can be used to do homework just as well with appropriate software and a good trip to the library. Parental popularity may not be big in such a home, but child safety is the greater value. Popularity will eventually come—as appreciation.

Managing the Internet means...

- Supervision - Keeping your computer in a common area where the screen can be easily seen by anyone in the room.
- Compiling a list of safe sites on your "Favorites" list your child is allowed to visit. This can be easily done

with the help of your local librarian and other parents.

- Supervising postings – Forms should never be filled out without your permission. When you give your permission, be there to make sure the form is on a "secure" site which prevents information from being viewed by other people. Personal information about your child or family should not be posted on the Internet.
- Screening e-mail - Until the age you choose, take a look at what is sent to your child. Forbid the opening of anything from a stranger.
- Investing in parental controls software.

Being a parent these days is a balancing act. We have to give children enough freedom to explore the world, but know when and how far to be vigilant.

When it comes right down to it, all the rules in the world cannot guarantee safety for our children. It's not just about the latest in screening software or blocking devices. It's about the kind of people we are and the atmosphere in which we raise children. Who we are on the inside and what we do when we're not online says a lot about what we'll do in a chat room. The kind of fiber we build in our children will largely determine their desires online.

I was watching Glen Beck interview Stephen Covey and his son the other night. I was fascinated by the quality of the son, his integrity and his insight into life. My thought was that if the fathers of this world would heed Stephen Covey's advice and raise the kind of sons he raised, we wouldn't be having the problems we're having. The root of much of the emptiness of young people today is simply the absence of involved parents.

Fortunately, Mr. Covey has written numerous books on the subject that are available to anyone with a library card.

My good friend Jane and her husband Michael are model 21st Century parents. Even I get a little tired of their diligence sometimes and wish they would just get a sitter and come with me to something-or-other where kids aren't welcome.

But they don't! They have two children, age nine and eleven who are watched like hawks and loved like puppies. Their house always has one or two extra kids around because Mike and Jane know that if their friends are welcome, Michael and Anna will be more content at home. They are forever running here or there with the kids because proper supervision is critical for them. It's not easy now, but will pay off in spades with healthy adulthoods.

If you suspect...

Most people talk themselves out of their suspicions. It's hard to approach a situation with confidence if there is no proof. If you suspect that something inappropriate may be happening, discuss it with someone you trust. Most importantly, talk to your child. Give him or her the security of being able to talk openly with you. There will be some behavioral changes in children who are being abused. Glenda spoke with me about her son:

> I was always puzzled about why my older son walked around with slumped shoulders and seemed depressed so much of the time. When he and my other boy would head out for the bus, he would walk straight ahead and not look back. My younger son would be smiling and waving and blowing kisses to me all the way out the driveway. It didn't make sense. My older son was handsome, smart, healthy and I thought he came from a great family. I dressed him as well as I could and tried to make life really special for him. He seemed angry with me so much of

> the time. I couldn't break through. Something was wrong and I didn't know what it was. Now I know. I failed to protect him because I didn't suspect he was in any danger.

If you have cause for suspicion, the most important thing is to talk with your child. There will be behavior changes in a child who is being abused.

There may be:

- Nightmares
- A new knowledge of sex related words
- A new fear of going somewhere he has been before, or seeing a person he knows
- Physical signs such as redness or injury in the genital or oral area
- Excessive masturbation or interest in playing games about sex
- Signs of emotional conflict within the child
- Depression
- Sleeping more than usual
- Poor posture
- Lack of self-esteem
- Difficulties with relationships
- Inability to concentrate
- Eating disorders
- Acting out
- Shoplifting or other delinquent behaviors
- Truancy or running away
- Use of alcohol or drugs
- A change in academic achievement
- Disconnection from the family

The most reliable way to determine whether your suspicions are valid is to have your child evaluated at a treatment centre that specializes in sexual abuse cases. It may be helpful to find a therapist knowledgeable in the field to work with the child on behavior issues until the child is ready to disclose the abuse.

If you, yourself, have been abused, it may be that you lack the objectivity to discern what is happening in your child's life. Your super sensitivity to the issue may be leading you to see abuse where there is none. Conversely, your emotions regarding the issue may lead you to avoid dealing with the problem. If you're confused, it's important to seek the advice of a professional well-acquainted with the issues.

It's impossible to be right about everything all the time. There may be times when you're wrong. The bottom line is that the best we can do is the best we can do to keep our children safe and to reassure them that they can come to us with anything that is bothering them.

If a child actually discloses the fact that he or she is being abused, believe it. While there are situations, usually in custody battles, where a parent will coach a child to accuse a parent of abuse, it's usually obvious. For a child to fake the trauma of an abuse victim, exhibiting the profound emotional reactions would be worthy of an Oscar.

Let the law deal with it

Without proof, denial is almost a sure thing from the suspect. Glenda continued:

> Not until he was 13-years-old, did my son feel big enough to start saying no to his abuser and tell my husband and me, in

another time of crisis, what he had been enduring for so many years. Only then did his demeanor all those years make sense.

When I arranged a meeting in a restaurant with the man who had victimized my son and confronted him with my son's disclosure, he appeared utterly shocked and said, "How could you even think such a thing?"

I said, "On top of everything you've done to my son and me, are you going to make him a liar, too?" With that, he looked down and admitted his guilt.

I now deeply regret the way I handled it from that point on.

It was the 80's and child sexual abuse was almost never in the news. I had no idea how to handle it and numbly tried to feel my way. No one I knew had ever had to face such a thing. I called the police anonymously and asked what would happen if I were to report it. Prior to that, I had never had any dealings with police beyond a speeding ticket. The idea of involving them in my life was foreign to me. When they said yes, that my son would probably be called to testify, I decided not to take that route but to handle it myself. I thought it would be terribly difficult for him to have to go through the court process. He had already been through so much and my entire mind-set was geared to protecting him from any further trauma.

And so I arranged the restaurant meeting, naïvely thinking that if I could just introduce the offender to God and have his life transformed, it would save my son the dreaded court process and accomplish more in the abuser's life than sitting in a jail cell could ever do. I saw the condition of his dark heart as the real problem and thought the most effective way of changing it was through spiritual transformation. So, after telling him that he would not be welcome in our home and could not see my sons again until he had made himself right with God, I sent him off with a Bible and some books I had purchased for him that I thought would speak to the situation.

> What I didn't understand at the time was the manipulative nature of the child molester. I was still the trusting little mommy who believed that things could really be the way they appeared.
>
> I am not saying that God could not have totally transformed that man's life. I have seen it happen over and over again in amazing ways. However, the person has to want to change with all their heart. Otherwise, God can't do the work.
>
> Naturally, my son's molester appeared after a couple of days of thinking about the situation and claimed to have had a spiritual conversion. At first, it appeared that I had done the right thing. I thought he was changed from the inside out. I thought all predatory inclinations had been washed away with the cleansing of his dark heart.
>
> Unfortunately, the real changes that should have happened with a genuine spiritual awakening didn't happen and as soon as the crisis appeared to be over, he reverted to his normal personality. Not long after, he developed cancer and died.

While God apparently looked after the situation in His own way, if Glenda had it to do again, she said she would definitely have involved the police. For one thing, it's the law. Child sexual abuse has to be reported. She, like many other naïve parents, didn't know that away back then.

Child molesters need to be punished. They need the chastisement of jail, the humiliation of walking in shackles to court, the embarrassment of donning the orange jumpsuit, the fear of the other inmates, the rudeness of the guards, the grief of losing their normal lives, the emptiness of losing control of everything, the time to think about what they have done to everyone whose shattered lives have touched theirs.

Victims need to feel that there has been some justice for all they have suffered.

While Glenda thought she was being so kind to her son by protecting him from further trauma, what really happened was that she denied him the opportunity to see justice done. That gave rise to a deep anger and sense of injustice within him. By the time she realized it, it was too late. It was more baggage that he had to sort through and carry. She wishes she could go back.

Community Protection

They say it takes a village to raise a child. In the same way, it takes a village to protect a child. While parents are the first line of defense for a child, organized community response is vital as an effective support to the parents' efforts.

Community efforts to protect against child abuse are being augmented by the fact that over the past 15 years, the issue of child abuse has become the single most important liability issue facing insurance companies in North America. Consequently, very few insurance agencies will insure organizations and institutions against allegations of abuse unless they can prove that they have a formal plan in place to ensure safety from child predators and that everything possible is being done to prevent such occurrences within the client's organization.

In Remembrance of Victoria

Melodie Bissell, President and CEO of Winning Kids Inc.®, wrote a blog in memory of a little girl who died at the hands of her guardians as the surrounding community turned a deaf ear.

> I came upon the story of Victoria, a little girl who was abused and murdered by her guardians in London, England in 2000. The public outrage at her death led to a public inquiry which produced major changes in child protection policies in the United Kingdom, including the formation of the *Every Child*

Matters program; the introduction of the Children's Act of 2004 and the creation of the *Contact Point Project*, a government database that holds any information regarding abuse on children in the UK.

At the time of her death, the numerous locations of lacerations on this wee girl's body were horrifying. Evidence showed that Victoria was beaten on a daily basis with a shoe, a coat hanger or a wooden cooking spoon and her abuser would strike her toes with a hammer. Victoria's blood was found on her uncle's football boots. He admitted that at times he would hit her with a bicycle chain.

In her post mortem it was found that Victoria had 128 separate injuries on her body. No area had been spared. Marks on her wrists and ankles indicated that her arms and legs had been tied together. It was the worst case of deliberate harm to a child the investigator had ever seen.

There were over 100 witnesses to Victoria's maltreatment and abuse. This was not done in secret. The community services, hospitals, doctors, social workers, teachers, babysitters, neighbours all had seen the injuries and suspected the abuse, but *waited for others to respond. The community did not join forces and respond.*

Weeks prior to Victoria's death, she was taken to a local church on two separate occasions. The pastor was told that she was demon possessed and need prayer. On both occasions, he prayed over her and encouraged her to be a good girl and obey everything her aunt and uncle instructed her to do.

This story is heart breaking; not only because of the senseless death of Victoria, but because so many community workers held key information which, if it had been shared and acted upon, could have spared her life.

Victoria was born days before my youngest daughter, Courtney was born. Courtney will be graduating from high school this year. If Victoria were alive today, she too might be graduating with her whole future ahead of her.

The account of Victoria Adjo Climbié's life continues to underscore the mission of *Winning Kids Inc*. Our desire is to put the tools and training for abuse recognition and prevention into the hands of community groups. We exist to bring understanding to those who work in schools, camps, churches, sporting leagues, babysitting, piano teaching, tutoring, counseling and all aspects of child interaction, regarding the critical nature of awareness and preparedness to protect children and youth.

Daily I read material on websites by individuals bashing churches, synagogues, schools and clergy for not protecting the children. We need to start working together on behalf of the most vulnerable in our society and applaud the great efforts that are being made daily.

It is alarming to continue to hear the stories of abuse. Unfortunately, we have a long way to go before we win the race against abuse. We will, however, accomplish much more if we work together to create a protective environment in our communities and be proactive in initiating healing communities.

Plan to Protect

Melodie, with her associates, has developed *Plan to Protect,* a protection manual for children, youth and churches. It has been used by over 3,500 organizations over the last ten years. She says:

At *Winning Kids Inc*., we believe the battle can be won through creating winning environments for children and youth. Our *Plan To Protect* program is a prevention plan aimed at the eradication of physical, sexual and emotional abuse of children and safeguarding them from neglect. We are committed to helping to prevent abuse in schools, churches, camps, daycares, clubs and in sports.

Our team has many decades of experience in creating safe environments for children. We have authored *Plan to Protect* which is now the protection plan being used in 3,500 churches, schools, associations and daycares. It is a comprehensive 250 page protection plan with policies, plans, training outlines, case studies, and 30+ appendices. This manual is laid out in a format that both the board and the leaders can easily use to establish a strong abuse prevention policy and program. The manual is widely used across the nation. Additionally, we can process Criminal Record Checks in order to provide further evidence that the organization is doing everything within its ability to show that "Child Protection" is in place.

Winning Kids Inc. has recently launched on-line training for *Plan to Protect.* When an acceptable score is achieved, demonstrating comprehension of the policies, a Certificate of Completion can be issued. They also have a service to provide customized policies.

Our programs and tools meet the seven key initiatives that are generally acknowledged by experts in establishing an effective formal abuse prevention plan and are required by insurance companies in order to qualify for abuse coverage:

- Statement of Policy
- Definition of Abuse
- Screening Procedures
- Operational Procedures
- Premise Modifications
- Annual and Ongoing Training
- Abuse Response Protocol

While our program will assist organizations and institutions in satisfying the requirements of insurance companies for abuse coverage, the primary motivation for keeping predators away from our children always has to be the safety of the children themselves.

Kenneth A. Hall, the president of Robertson Hall Insurance Inc., says this about *Plan To Protect:*

> For over a decade Robertson Hall Insurance has recommended *Plan To Protect* to our church client organizations. The updated version for 2007 is even more user-friendly, practical and understandable for church and charity leaders as they seek effective ways to protect the children and youth in their care against potential harm and protect their ministry workers from false allegations. Plenty of great examples, training ideas and sample forms means that your organization doesn't have to reinvent the wheel when it comes to abuse prevention. Having the new edition and updated materials as a resource and template for abuse prevention policies and procedures is like the benefit of an expert without having one in your congregation. We applaud the efforts of Melodie Bissell and *Winning Kids* for making effective abuse prevention more understandable and achievable ..."

Lorna Dueck, journalist and host of *Listen Up TV* recently wrote an article encouraging the use of the *Plan To Protect*. She said:

> The story of *Plan to Protect* is one I strongly believe in. At a time when newspapers are inundated with stories of school, organization, league and church payouts to victims in the billions of dollars, there are individuals committed to creating safe environments for children. My own church is one of them! We have been using *Plan to Protect* for the past decade. It has become a priceless tool.
>
> *Plan to Protect* includes the guidelines and structure to minimize the opportunities for child abuse to occur. Organizations in Canada working among children and youth are rising to the challenge and implementing policies and procedures to ward off predators. I would like to believe our children are now safe, but the stories of abuse continue to be reported. Many a tear falls from Heaven every time a child is abused. This week, this month, this year, tears continue to fall; crime stories continue to fill our airwaves. Predators are only a mouse click away.

Predator-Proofing our Children

The story needs to be told of those who are screening out the predators, and providing protection so that our children cannot only survive but thrive. We cannot rest on our laurels; we must continually strive to protect children one at a time....

Ever before us are the stories of caregivers, teachers, coaches and clergy who set aside their pledge to mentor and have robbed children of their innocence. Is God silent? I believe God is not silent when it comes to abuse but has spoken harshly against those that cause children to suffer. I also believe He hears the cries of the oppressed and victimized and has called together a community of defenders who will be his arms and feet to free the burdened and battered. You too may be one of those defenders protecting our children in schools, camps, daycares, churches and clubs. I encourage you to not let your efforts fall flat; do not let down your guard. You too have a part to play in this plan to protect!

Hats off to the authors of *Plan to Protect* and the founders of *Winning Kids Inc.*, who give us the tools to cherish and protect the most valuable asset we have, children!

Predators in Pews and Pulpits

Thousands of child sex abuse cases never see newspaper ink. What happens in schools, hockey rinks, families, camps or shopping malls, is most often shrouded in secrecy.

However, when a church member or one of the clergy is involved in an abuse case, the ink runs from the front page to the back. The salacious value is always higher when what is supposed to be good shows up as evil. It makes more of a story when the shock and liability leads to Rome or the apexes of other denominations which have established themselves as the purveyors of morality and the enemies of sin.

Nevertheless, it's not the press that's causing the crisis in the church: it's people who have put themselves in positions of ultimate trust, betraying the faithful by taking advantage of the most vulnerable. In the Catholic Church alone, over a billion dollars has been paid out to victims for clergy malfeasance, to say nothing of monies spent on legal services. A study commissioned by the U.S. Bishops and carried out under the direction of the John Jay College of Criminal Law, was released in February of 2004. The conclusion was that between three and six percent of priests are abusers of minors. That's about one in twenty. The crisis is home grown.

When a child is abused by someone in the church, perhaps even by a family member, it often destroys any faith the child has or might otherwise have developed. Sitting in a pew watching the molester raising his hands to God and singing "Hallelujah," Sunday after Sunday, makes a child doubt the integrity of every man there. Why wouldn't it? Even solid, genuine men of God are at risk of being tarred with the same brush in the mind of an abused child. On the outside, they all look the same. Why would the child think any of them would be different on the inside?

Philosopher/theologian Martin Buber shared this insight in M. Scott Peck's *People of the Lie*:[40]

> "Since the primary motive of the evil is disguise, one of the places evil people are most likely to be found is within the church. What better way to conceal one's evil from oneself, as well as from others, than to be a deacon or some other highly visible form of Christian within our culture? . . . . I do not mean to imply that the evil are anything other than a small minority among the religious or that the religious motives of most people are in any way spurious. I mean only that evil people tend to gravitate toward piety for the disguise and concealment it can offer them."

The sad truth is that if it looks like a duck, walks like a duck and quacks like a duck—these days it's not always a duck.

40. M. Scott Peck (1983). People of the Lie, New York, Touchstone - Simon & Schuster Inc.

Double whammy

The tragic thing is that those who claim to be Christians and then are exposed as pedophiles can devastate the faith of others, particularly those who are young and impressionable or who base their faith on the performance of those who call themselves Christians.

Those upon whom they prey receive a double whammy—the results of their abuse *plus* the possible loss of the very thing that should be of the greatest help in their restoration—their faith.

People will always let others down. The only one who ever lived the Christian life the way it's supposed to be lived was Jesus. The example of everyone else is flawed to greater or lesser degrees and falls short of perfection. Those who depend on the examples of other people to affirm their faith are doomed to disappointment and probable loss of their faith.

Victims who lose their faith lose not only their childhoods, but possibly a happy eternity. When that happens, the offender has committed them not only to a life of baggage, but also to an afterlife of separation from God. The victim will be responsible for choosing bitterness over faith and forgiveness because in the end, we will all be responsible for our own choices—even those made very difficult by the evil actions of others.

The iHeart?

It used to be that church-going people seemed like a pretty good lot. The majority of them still are. But the issue is not whether or not one goes to church; it's what is in one's heart. And therein lies the problem. When a person walks in a church door, there's no electronic scanner to prove that the outward appearance matches the heart. There's no device to guarantee that the person sitting beside one in a pew is trustworthy.

Such a device might not be a bad idea! Since the apple was the first symbol of sin, we could call it the iHeart! Congregants could enter through an electronically designed metal arch which would identify the state of each person's heart. From there, they could be streamed into a variety of rooms tailored for ministry according to their specific needs: beep beep—black hearts downstairs for Transformation Ministry; beep—white hearts upstairs for Leadership Instruction; beep, beep, beep—grey hearts to the left for a course on Apologetics; beep, beep, beep, beep—yellow hearts to the right for a Christian Courage seminar; low beep—blue hearts to the altar for Deliverance from Depression; no beep—empty hearts to the office to sign a pedophile permission contract before joining the black hearts downstairs for Transformation Ministry.

Life could be so much simpler with a machine like that. However, we live in a world where we have to play guessing games about what kind of hearts lie inside our neighbors. Where discernment is lacking, danger can hide.

Contemporary society is sick and is producing more and more sick individuals. The church—hospitals for the transformation of hearts—should be the best place for them, if only the leaders and congregants would take its teachings to heart.

The porn factor

Chapter Five, "The Porn Factor," details the enormous influence pornography has wrought on society. Once a dirty little secret, it has become an epidemic. Countless men and women of all ages, professions and nationalities, whether Christian leaders or athiests, are admitting they struggle personally with pornography. Unfortunately, people who sit in church pews or stand behind pulpits are within reach of its tentacles.

Scott Covington, CEO & Executive Director of Net Accountability, (a ministry providing research, reach and resources for a revolution toward sexual purity)[41] and Curt Swindoll, CEO of Cool Strategies (a consultancy which works with mission-minded organizations in the areas of strategic planning, business development, organizational leadership, and marketing)[42] wrote a paper entitled, "Pornography: No Longer a Dirty Little Secret." In it, they demonstrated the inroads pornography has made into the Christian community with the following facts:

- Over 50 percent of evangelical pastors report they viewed pornography last year.
- 34 percent of female readers of Today's Christian Woman's online newsletter admitted to intentionally accessing Internet porn in a recent poll.
- Pornography is a $10 billion business - bigger than the NFL, NBA and Major League Baseball combined.
- 50 percent of Promise Keepers attendees viewed porn within a week before the event.
- One of 10 respondents to a recent MSNBC.com poll said they are "sexually addicted" to Internet pornography.

---

41. scott@netaccountability.com
42. curt@coolstrategies.com

- 20 percent of the Internet consists of pornographic content.
- 300,000,000 x-rated videos were distributed in the US-more than the entire US population - and that was 13 years ago.
- Hollywood releases 11,000 adult movies per year - more than 20 times mainstream movie production.
- One in five children (age 10-17) have received unwanted sexual solicitations online
- 1800 percent - pornography growth over the last five years.

Scott and Curt go on to say:

> No longer simply someone else's problem, pornography has invaded the hearts and homes of your family and friends, and most likely your church. The good news is the battle isn't over! But overcoming it requires that you understand it and take action.
>
> Those struggling with pornography, whether occasionally or daily, deal with the issue in one of two ways. Some live life telling themselves, "...I can stop anytime I choose". Rather than confront the demon proactively, they treat it with silence and a bold determination that next time they're tempted, they'll win. But experience and statistics are not on their side.
>
> Others have given up the fight by rationalizing their involvement. After all, what's the harm in looking at a few pictures, or in renting an explicit video on occasion? They've tossed aside scriptural teaching focusing on the importance of moral purity, just as some denominations have rationalized their position on homosexuality.
>
> But regardless of their response, playing with porn is playing with fire. Consider the findings of the LAPD Sexually Exploited Child (SEC) Unit. The LAPD-SEC examined the relationship

between extra-familial child abuse and pornography in their cases over a ten-year period, dating from 1980-1989. Their findings are startling.

Pornography was directly involved in 62 percent of the cases they reviewed and actually recovered in 55 percent of their cases. The study's author concludes: "Clearly, pornography, whether it be adult or child pornography, is an insidious tool in the hands of the pedophilic population... The study merely confirms what detectives have long known: that pornography is a strong factor in the sexual victimization of children."

The New Crack Cocaine

According to Dr. James Dobson, Internet pornography is the new "Crack Cocaine." Addiction can be swift, giving users progressively increasing desire for more and increasingly perverted material. Just as drug users experience a "high" with their drugs of choice, pornography addicts experience a similar "high" as the brain releases endorphins and an intense feeling of euphoria results, leading to deeper addiction.

While not all users of pornography become molesters of children, the reality is that none of them intended to sink that low when they logged onto their first porn site. None of them envisioned losing homes, families, professions or societal acceptability when they saw those first raunchy images.

Unlike cocaine users, however, porn addicts have a constant, 24 hour a day supply of their drug available in the safety of their own homes with just a click of a mouse. Priests, ministers, rabbis, parishioners all have X-rated porn shops right in their own homes if they are hooked up to the internet. They don't have to fear having their reputations ruined by been seen covertly buying skin magazines.

Why do pedophiles go to church?

The majority of pedophiles don't go to church, but those who do occupy pews for a variety of reasons.

While there are those who go specifically because they see it as a fertile field for growing relationships with children and their families, others are there as part of family groups who regularly attend, more from tradition than from any sincere spiritual interest.

Still others go to church because they want help, but don't confront their perversions with counseling because they fear exposure. They're hoping God will supernaturally zap them like a celestial Mr. Fixit. They're open to using Him for their own benefit, but they're not necessarily interested in a relationship with Him.

And then there are those who are there because they have experienced legitimate encounters with God. Their lives have been transformed to a certain degree and they have a desire to walk in their faith, but, lacking total commitment, they have allowed old thought-patterns to occupy more and more space until their faith is more a cover than a reality. Gradually giving free rein to their perverted thoughts, their inappropriate desires outweigh the importance of God in their lives.

The God factor

In the course of researching this series, I interviewed the family of Matt, a convicted molester who, it would appear, belonged to the latter group. They claimed that he had a genuine change in his life at the time of his conversion in 1978. The whole situation was not only devastating for them, but very confusing because they were all adamant that he could not have sustained the changes in his character and personality for such a long time, had his conversion not been real. It was four years later that he had an encounter with a young girl who exposed her breasts to him. The moment that he reached out to touch her, was the moment in time that changed all of their lives forever. With one touch of his hand to her breast, they became the family of a child molester.

Just as in story after story, the father of this family had indulged in pornography as a young boy and continued his addiction into his adult years. I believe that the pornography was like a bag of weed seed continuously scattered over more than a dozen years of Matt's life. When he became a Christian, the bag was thrown away, but the roots with which the pornography had gripped his heart were not ripped out. They remained dormant until fertile conditions emerged for them to bear fruit.

The Bible talks a lot about confession of sins and repentance. These are old-fashioned words that we don't hear much anymore, except in sarcasm. But I'm going to use them here because they're uniquely applicable to the topic of this chapter. There's no better word than *sin* to identify thoughts or behavior contrary to the precepts of the Bible. *Repentance* is much more than an apology for sin. It involves a total turning away from the particular thoughts or behaviors, towards alignment with God's principles. It's easy to apologize, but only meaningful when it holds the commitment to change—the essence of repentance.

In Matt's life, that would have meant recognizing pornography and abnormal sexual desires as unacceptable aspects of his life. The repentance part would have meant ripping out the roots by exposing them and disallowing them any space in his psyche or behavior.

Sometimes, the identification with sins of various kinds is so deep that it requires particularly intense focus in the process of rejection of those inclinations or behaviors. Many Christians are sloppy in their faith and don't understand how important it is to make sure that no vestiges remain of sins which, if allowed to remain, could cause problems down the road.

The problem with thoughts like sexual perversion is pride. If a person is afraid of what people will think if he or she admits to having thoughts that deviate from the norm, it will be difficult to deal with them in any kind of realistic way. Shame often prevents a person from the necessary freedom of transparency. Without admitting to weaknesses of the heart, there can be no accountability, leaving the person in grave risk of acting on his or her weaknesses.

In an Alcoholics Anonymous meeting, the first step to recovery is finding the willingness to stand up and say, "I am John Doe and I am an alcoholic." If society would allow people to confess their inappropriate sexual thoughts in a ministry setting, it would benefit from the structure of accountability that could be put in place before a child suffers from the person's progression from fantasy to acting upon the fantasies.

Many people have the idea that some sins are okay while others are unforgiveable. I have a feeling that when God looks at sin in a person's life, he just sees a black stain. There are no shades of the rainbow. Things are either acceptable or unacceptable. He says that if we recognize and admit to the unacceptable aspects of our lives (sins) and reject them, He will not only forgive them, but will forget about them.

Unfortunately, humans aren't always so forgiving. If someone confesses publicly to something like thoughts of pedophilia and asks God for forgiveness, there are those who will be all over the "news" like tabloid reporters (asking others to pray for the person, of course). Knowing what some church people can be like, can make it almost impossible for someone with inappropriate sexual thoughts to deal with them before their thoughts catapult into actions.

Meanwhile, those who most vehemently reject pedophiles, or other kinds of sex addicts, are often messed up in their own lives with junk piles of all forms of self-indulgences.

God highly values humility over pride and requires repentance before forgiveness can be experienced.

So there it is. That's the struggle of the pedophile in the pew. "Do I get my thoughts cleaned up with God before I hurt somebody—or do I try to maintain my dignity by appearing to be a normal, healthy Christian and continue to rot inside, risking eventual acting out?"

After speaking with his family, I interviewed Matt.

D. After you became a Christian, I understand that the pornography stopped – and yet you say that it was a factor in you becoming a child molester.

M. It did stop for awhile. I'm guessing for seven or eight years.

D. So your faith in God didn't do anything to put an end to those desires?

M. It certainly did for awhile, but then I think I just slid back. It became all about self-gratification again.

D. Did you ever try to seek help in any way?

M. Yes. I would constantly pray that the Lord would get me out of it. I knew it was wrong and felt very guilty after the fact, but just wasn't strong enough to stop it.

D. So if you prayed that God would help you to stop, why do you think He didn't?

M. I think it was just a hollow prayer. It just wasn't sincere. My desire for what I was doing was stronger than my desire to stop.

D. What about your relationship with God. Do you feel that you had an authentic Christian conversion in 1978?

M. Yes. It was authentic. But I slid backwards. I had committed my life to God and believed everything in the Bible. I just wasn't following what it said. I put my own desires ahead of everything and didn't work at applying Scripture to my life. I was just a guy sitting in a pew saying all the right things but doing whatever I felt like doing.

Did you feel as though God had left you in prison?

M. No, although I certainly deserved to have Him leave me. There were so many occurrences when really bad things could have happened. I could have died. Just on my pod there were several guys who would have killed me as quick as they would have looked at me if they could have gotten their hands on me. I feel that God gave me wisdom in what to say, what to do and how to react. Whenever I would ask Him what I was to do in a particular situation, I would just feel a flood of peace and I knew He was with me. I'd do whatever it was I felt He told me to do and I was protected.

D. How has your relationship with Him changed?

M. He is all I have now. I came to terms with Him before I went to jail, at the same time that I determined that I had to do the right thing and confess. Ever since, I've felt that there are no walls between me and God. I can be real with Him.

D. What would you say to all those men who are sitting in church pews or living otherwise respectable lives but logging on to porn sites when no one is around?

M. They need some accountability. They need people around them who can bring them up on the carpet on anything. And those men they want to select very carefully. A man needs an accountability group around him until the day he dies—at least one man, preferably two or more.

That's where I have been so blessed with Jack and Tom and Derek. I talk to Derek at least three times a week, sometimes more and they ask me the hard questions. Jack and I are in the process of setting up some accountability software that enables accountability partners (us) to mail eachother their internet history for each week. It's a great tool that more men should use.

D. How did you sit in church on Sundays and listen to Christian radio and yet maintain your interest in pornography?

M. Again, the self gratification outweighed my spiritual walk. I was weak spiritually. I think every man has the potential for giving in to pornography and if they do, they just gradually deteriorate. It may take hours, days, weeks, months or years—but if you play with fire, you're going to get burned.

I believe the only way to stay clear is by feeding on the actual Word of God. Listening to great preachers or reading books may be good, but that's not it. It can be helpful—Dr. Stanley really helped me from time to time. But there's nothing that replaces the Word of God. Philippians, Chapter Four, was very important to me. It's like the oil that makes everything work right. If you can stay grounded in Scripture, you have hope. It's the key to success. If you try to wean away from it, you're in trouble. It's got to be first place. It's got to be priority job one. Knowing that for the rest of your life is extremely important. It gives a peace that you can't get anywhere else.

D. How about the contention that people in your circumstances just get "jailhouse religion?"

M. That's often true. Many of the fellows in prison had exactly that. Their visits to the chaplain were all about ulterior motives. They wanted to be regarded well by parole boards or whatever. I knew when I was writing some of those letters for them that I was being used—so for those people I tried to write even better letters, because it wasn't my job to judge their hearts. God has a purpose. While I was in there, I was supposed to help those fellows in any way I could. I did everything I could for them.

Flawed doctrine—or flawed people?

How can a person preach from a pulpit or sit in a pew listening to scripture, year after year, and then molest a child? Two behaviors could not be more divergent. Are the teachings of Jesus flawed?

There's nothing wrong with Jesus or His teachings. He partook of the human experience, offered the ultimate sacrifice, conquered death and provided a Life Manual (the Bible) as a guidebook to get people through this life into the next one.

The problem is not one of corrupt, irrelevant doctrine, but of individuals who refuse to participate in God's teachings His way. They're willing to live the Christian life as far as it doesn't interfere in what they really want to do or how they really want to live, but they treat the Bible like a smorgasbord—choosing the morsels that appeal to them and ignoring or rejecting the rest. If clergy or parishioners, regardless of denomination, were faithful to the teachings of the church, none of them would abuse children.

The phenomenon of child sexual abuse in association with a church setting is one of sick individuals using their spiritual or moral authority to prey on children. While man-made traditions surrounding the teachings of Scripture can contribute to sexual dysfunctions, child sexual abuse is a practice in absolute opposition to the content of the teachings.

The mind of the predator in church

What goes through the mind of a predator sitting in a pew, listening to a sermon on the consequences of sin?

Or what if the predator is the one who has prepared and is delivering the message? How does that work? How does the message of the Bible fit in a brain preoccupied with child molestation?

Religion is nothing but structure. One can be religious about making one's bed in the morning or about following a healthy diet. It's just a belief system and doesn't necessarily have anything to do with God.

Religion as it applies to the Bible, applies structure to the application of the precepts laid out in it. Unfortunately, many, many people pay more attention to the structure than the precepts. The medium is not the message.

If a person adheres to the structure of religion through following church traditions, they can fool themselves into some sort of whacky justification, thinking that their association with an institution that offers forgiveness gives them immunity to guilt.

People don't become real Christians by going to church every week any more than they become lions by visiting the zoo every week—or become steaks when they visit a steak house.

The God presented in the Bible is very much a supernatural entity whose ways are very different than natural ways of thinking and doing things. Without entering into that supernatural realm through experiencing an actual spiritual rebirth, religion is just another exercise.

Priests, Ministers or Rabbis—who's real?

In recent years, the Catholic Church has been rocked all the way to Rome with horrendous stories of abuse perpetrated by fatherly priests. Until now, it has been difficult to assess the Protestant situation because Protestant churches are not as centralized as the Catholic Church.

Out of the spotlight glare, Protestants have self-righteously read their daily issues of *The Pharisee Times*, thinking, "Oh I'm so glad I'm not one of *them*."

That is, until a report came out in the Insurance Journal, June 18, 2007, citing figures from the three companies that insure the majority of Protestant churches in the U.S.A.: Church Mutual Insurance Co., GuideOne Insurance Co. and Brotherhood Mutual Insurance Co. Together, these three companies insure well over half of the 224,000 Protestant churches recognized by the Association of Statisticians of American Religious Bodies.

These three companies claim to receive over 260 reports each year of minors under the age of 18 being abused by either a member of the clergy or someone in the church. (While Brotherhood Mutual Insurance Co. receives an average of 73 reports per year, they have not broken it down to indicate how many of those are under the age of 18, and so they are not included in the 260 reports.)

According to Father Jonathan Morris, a columnist for Fox News, The Catholic Church has reported that since 1950, about 228 credible accusations per year have been brought against Catholic clerics.

While the Catholics would no doubt feel some relief if the scores were somehow evened out, these aren't really the kind of numbers one wants to see matched or bettered. However, if, as they claim, most incidents of abuse are committed by married men, celibacy may not be the issue it was once thought to be.

It's very difficult to get accurate numbers with so many variables. Besides the fact that the numbers for the Protestant churches are representative of only half of the churches, the time span which the Catholics use for averaging, holds its own myriad of variables.

Once again, we have to go to the bottom line, which is that if one child were sexually abused by a cleric or congregant, whether Catholic, Protestant, Jewish, Muslim, Buddhist or Martian, it would be reprehensible. It would be one child too many. The problem of child sexual abuse has no denominational boundaries.

Clerics of all persuasions are in positions of unique responsibility and privilege. They are charged with leading those in their charge through this life to the next.

> "...offenses will come: but woe unto him through whom they come. It were better for him that a millstone were hanged around his neck, and he cast into the sea, than that he should offend one of these little ones." (Luke 17:1b-2)[43]

> "Inasmuch as ye have done it unto one of the least of these my brethren, ye have done it unto me." (Matthew 25:40)[44]

In response to the shocking figures, according to the insurance companies, churches are working harder to prevent child sexual abuse by conducting background checks, installing windows in nurseries and play areas and requiring at least two adults in a room with a child. Some are working toward a national database of ministers who have been credibly accused of, personally confessed to, or legally have been convicted of sexual harassment or abuse. The goal is to break the code of silence and to have complete transparency when allegations are raised.

Joe Trull, editor of *Christian Ethics Today* and retired ethics professor at New Orleans Baptist Theological Seminary, quoted in the June, 2007 issue of *The Insurance Journal*, said, "We're going to have to become more proactive and let (churches) know if they don't come forward, they're helping to perpetuate this problem."

While the protection of children should always be the primary motivation for putting a plan in place to ensure the safety of children, the fact that the issue of child abuse has become the single most important liability issue facing insurance companies in North America has forced groups to do something about the

43. Luke 17:1b-2, The Holy Bible, King James Version
44. Matthew 25:40, The Holy Bible, King James Version

situation. Very few insurance agencies will insure organizations and institutions against allegations of abuse unless they can prove that they have a formal plan in place to ensure safety from child predators and that everything possible is being done to prevent such occurrences within the client's organization.

SNAP

SNAP (Survivors Network of Those Abused by Priests) was formed in response to the need of abuse victims for a support group. Like participants in 12-step meetings, the groups believe that sharing their embarrassing, confidential information helps those who have been abused by trusted members of the clergy, become coping survivors.

While institutions like the Catholic Church have invested in counseling for many of the known victims, they have offered little in terms of personal support. Apologies to victims are routinely made through press statements, but seldom with personal contact. This is partially due to the fact that individual diocese hesitate to interact with people pursuing litigation against them.

In the words of one SNAP organizer, "I'm here because I care for the people....We have to help each other. It's a shame, because it's the very principle (the Catholic Church) stands for. I don't think that if Jesus were here that he would ignore us. I think he would do whatever he could to make this right."

Sexual abuse in the church is nothing new

In 1741, Pope Benedict XIV published, "Sacramentum Poenitentiae," an apostolic constitution. It is a four-page document that deals with the issue of Roman Catholic priests soliciting sex from people, including children, during confession. It was an integral part of the canon-law book that was used to train all priests between 1918 and 1982. A convenient tool for lawyers to demonstrate the invalidity of claims by church officials that they were unaware of occurrences of abuse, the document has regularly found its way into legal battles surrounding the sexual abuse of children by the Catholic clergy.

The godly majority

While sexual abuse in the church is nothing new, neither is the presence of many, many godly men and women who have served God and man faithfully throughout the generations of time. While inappropriate actions can scar people for a lifetime, the example of genuine faith and selfless Christian service can leave a tremendously valuable, indelible mark on the life of a young person.

While one out of twenty priests (or a percentage of men in any denomination) may be abusers of children, nineteen out of twenty make a tremendously valuable contribution to society. We just have to make sure that our children don't run into "the one" and that if he is recognized, he is punished and dealt with in the most constructive way.

Redeeming the Church as a place for healing

The fact is that churches, like almost every other institution under the sun, have not been exempt from the dark deeds of child-molesters. The question is, beyond dealing with individual incidents as they arise, "What can the church do to minister to those who have been harmed behind its doors?"

Melodie Bissell, President of *Winning Kids Inc.*, the organization that developed the *Plan to Protect*, recently addressed a conference on how abuse affects the spirituality of children. She proposed *The Healing Circle* as a model whereby the church can most effectively partner with those who surround the child in the process of healing – the family, school, social services, therapists, friends and legal systems – for an integrated, wholistic approach to ministering to the victim; working together to accompany the child on the road to recovery. The following is an adaptation from her paper.

The Healing Circle

By Melodie Bissell, President, Winning Kids Inc.

The issue of abuse has rapidly become a leading area of concern for organizations responsible for the care and safely of children. Newspapers are filled with stories of payouts in the billions of dollars compensating victims who have been exploited by clergy. Religious institutions are being questioned as to their efforts to protect the vulnerable in their midst. "The issue of abuse...is now the single most important issue facing insurance companies."[45]

The call for abuse prevention seemingly distracts from the mission of the church.

But does it really?

Study after study shows that abuse has a tremendous impact on the stability and formation of spirituality in victims. The church

45. Ken Hall, Robertson Hall Insurance

must be redeemed as a place for healing rather than eyed with suspicion as a potential place for abuse. It must pro-actively contribute to restoration.

We need to introduce a model wherein the Christian church can nurture spiritual healing and wholeness as an integral part of a child's community – and that is what the *Winning Kids Inc. Healing Circle* is all about!

In order to position *The Healing Circle* in its necessary place of importance, we need to establish our focus within the broad understanding of "spirituality," define what we mean by "abuse" and understand its spiritual impact on childhood.

Parameters of Spirituality

While spirituality has been defined widely as "the personal truths that individuals hold as inviolable in their lives," we need to know how abuse impacts:

1. A child's belief in a higher being, a God who is holy, sovereign and loving;
2. A child's response to identifying with a community of believers; and
3. A child's spiritual formation as it relates to their purpose for living and hope for the future.

Child Abuse Defined

The Children's Aid Society of London and Middlesex has adopted the following definition of abuse: "Child abuse refers to an act committed by a parent, caregiver or person in a position of trust which is not accidental and which harms or threatens to harm a child's physical or mental health or a child's welfare...

The Healing Circle
Church
Medical / Counseling
Family
Legal
Friends
SCHOOL BUS STOP AHEAD
School
Social Services
Winning Kids®
www.winningkidsinc.ca
Rebuilding the walls of protection

abuse is primarily categorized as physical, sexual, emotional, or involving neglect."

The Spiritual Impact of Childhood Abuse

Child abuse is a phenomenon that sadly impacts millions of children. Considerable attention has been paid to the immediate and long term effects of abuse notably in relation to the impact on psycho-social functioning. Few studies, however, have focused on what may be called the spiritual impact of childhood abuse, despite the devastating consequences abuse has to the child's perception of, and relationship with, God.

According to Marilyn Ganje-Fling[46] and Patricia McCarthy, many of their clients who have been traumatized by sexual abuse, have experienced questions and conflicts regarding their spirituality. While many strive to relate to a powerful, higher being, they also struggle with a sense of hopelessness, the lack of a sense of purpose, and ambivalence about connecting with community.

Thomas Turrell's study[47] supports the observation that most psychological practice ignores the spiritual concerns of Christian victims and how these concerns influence psychological aspects of one's life. His study found that 60 percent of victims report an increased need for spirituality following the abuse – indicating that religion and spirituality can greatly impact victim recovery.

Though few studies have been done to determine the spiritual

46. Ganje-Fling, M. A., McCarthy, P.R. (1996). Impact of Childhood Sexual Abuse on Client Spiritual Development: Counseling Implications. Journal of Counseling and Development, 74, 253-258. Retrieved February 20, 2009 from Scholars Portal.

47. Turrell, S.C. Thomas, C.R. (2001). Where Was God? Utilizing Spirituality with Christian Survivors of Sexual Abuse. Women and Therapy, 24 (3-4) , 133-147. Retrieved February 3, 2009 from Scholars Portal.

impact of child abuse (physical/sexual/emotion), virtually all of the recorded studies show a negative effect spiritually. Most of the studies have been done by female (not children) survivors of sexual abuse. A significant impact consistently noted is a sense of spiritual alienation.

David Pelzer in his first book *A Child Called It*[48] speaks of his perception of God as it developed through his abusive childhood. The book is a horrific, first-person account of one of the most severe cases of child abuse in North America. Dave was brutally beaten and starved by his own mother. In the chapter "The Lord's Prayer," he writes: "About a month before I entered the fifth grade, I came to believe that for me, there was no God. … No just God would leave me like this. I believed that I was alone in my own struggle and my battle was one of survival."

In the movie *Deliver Us From Evil,* a documentary of the abuse within the Roman Catholic Church, testimony after testimony comes forth from victims who have been abused at the hands of priests. They indicate they will never re-enter a church because in their eyes this was God abusing them.

Rossetti, in the journal article, "The Impact of Child Sexual Abuse on Attitudes Toward God and the Catholic Church,[49]" reports the outcome of his study which focused on the abuse in Catholic churches and its correlation with the victims views on Church leadership, assessment of the church's response to child sexual abuse, evaluation of the church, trust in priests,

---

48. Pelzer, Dave (1995). *A Child Called "It"*: One Child's Courage to Survive. Deerfield Beach, Florida: Heath Communications.

49. Rossetti, S.J. (1995). The Impact of Child Sexual Abuse on Attitudes Toward God and the Catholic Church. Child Abuse and Neglect, 19(12), 1469-1481. Retrieved February 3, 2009 from Scholars Portal.

and relationship to God. He found that, "adults sexually abused as children by Catholic priests reported significantly less trust in the Catholic priesthood and church and in their relationship with God."

In the 2007 journal, *Scientific Study of Religion*[50], Gall, Basque, Damasceno-Scott. and Vardy focused on both the effect abuse has on spirituality and the effect spirituality has on coping with abuse. Their findings demonstrate that spiritual beliefs can be a positive force of treatment. This study mentioned many positives of spirituality, such as protection against depression and shame, support, aid in understanding, inner strength, self-acceptance, belonging and attachment. It also found that victims of child sexual abuse "reported having a negative image of God as being cruel, uncaring, and punishing" and "reported lower levels of spiritual well-being."

Diane Langberg, Ph.D. in her article, "The Spiritual Impact of Child Abuse," identifies why spiritual blocks and/or obstacles are formed. The first block is formed when the thought processes of a survivor appear to be "frozen" in time. For instance, a woman who was chronically abused by her father for 15 years thinks about herself, her life and her relationships through the grid of abuse. Trauma impedes growth because it shuts everything down. It brings death. Regardless of input from positive experiences, the thinking that originated within the context of the abuse is not altered. So – a woman who may have encountered many trustworthy people since her childhood

50. Gall, T.L., Basque, V., Damasceno-Scott, M., Vardy, G. (2007). Spirituality and the Current Adjustment of Adult Survivors of Childhood Sexual Abuse. Journal for the Scientific Study of Religion, 46(1) , 101-117. Retrieved February 3, 2009 from Scholars Portal.

abuse, may still have difficulties with trust. No matter how many thousands of words may be spoken about how God loves her, she may still feel worthless and that she is an exception to that truth. It may be true for others, but not for her.

The second block may be formed as a result of the immaturity of thought formations. Because child abuse is processed by a child's mind (children think concretely, not abstractly), abstract concepts of things like trust, truth and love may be warped from concrete experiences with significant others in their lives.

The third block may be built as a result of the fact that children (like adults) learn about the unseen (the spiritual) by way of the seen. God often teaches us eternal truths through the natural world. For instance, we learn about the shortness of life by the sudden disappearance of a vapor. Jesus taught through parables and parallels to life. He said that He was bread, light, water and a vine. As God in the flesh, He was an example of understanding the unseen through the seen. God continually brings eternal truths to us in ways we can understand. When relationships are marked by perversion, the child's understanding of God may become perverted through the experience of perversion.

While these and other studies give insight into the negative impact of abuse on spirituality, many testimonials point to the importance of spirituality in the healing process.

In her book, *Abuse Buster: The Second Step*, Billye Graham Bowman shares with readers her own story of abuse and the years she lived in darkness, suppressing her memories, without the knowledge of God's unconditional love. Once found, the love transformed her life. In her experience, one of the most important keys to finding healing was reading Scripture.

M. Galea, in *The Impact of Child Abuse on the Psycho-Spiritual and Religious Status of Maltese College Students*[51], while studying the negative effects of child abuse, gives insight into why spirituality plays an important role in the treatment of child abuse. "Suffering stimulates the need for meaning because people analyze and question their suffering far more than their joys." Because beliefs (such as religious beliefs) counteract hopelessness, they play an important part in the treatment process.

The Importance of Therapy

As abuse has long-term impact on a child, it is critical that long term counselling be provided. Short term pastoral care/counselling is often not enough to deal with the deep scars that a child may develop. It is important for a church to be prepared to immediately make referrals to therapists who they know will really minister to the needs of a child.

Competent Christian counselling by a trained therapist / psychologist or psychiatrist will begin to help a child deal with the God factor and minister to a child's spirituality in light of the abuse. The church can come alongside the family and child to provide pastoral care while the child is in therapy. This becomes a concrete example to the child that God is not silent.

Cheryl Ettinger, founder and President of House of Hope, is a highly trained psycho-therapist who participates in group support. She stresses the importance of securing a counselor for the child as soon after the trauma as possible. "Many adults

---

51. Galea, M. (2008). The Impact of Child Abuse on the Psycho-Spiritual and Religious Status of Maltese College Students. Pastoral Psychology, 57(3-4), 147-159. Retrieved February 3, 2009 from Scholars Portal.

believe that because children are resilient, they don't need as much support. Adults hope the children will forget it. They don't forget! They stay there and then years later they will pick it up again and only then will you see how angry they are at God. They may look like they are doing fine, so the decision is made not to send the child to a professional counselor. We do not count the spiritual cost of the crisis. While it is true children often bounce back, years later the pain from their past re-surfaces – if it has not been properly addressed. Even with childhood counseling, in adulthood they will raise the question, 'Why did God allow this to happen to me?'"

Cheryl encourages the children to "be the teacher." The child can teach adults how to interpret the abuse that happened, making them better equipped to be effective in their roles as parents, teachers, counselors or pastors. As a therapist, Cheryl may ask, "What is it like to be you?" Children are comfortable with being in the teacher role. "Healing begins to happen when you tell your story. Encourage the child to tell their story."

Theophostic therapists try to help the child see that Jesus is present within the counselling and is leading the way for truth to replace the darkness. The word "theophostic" comes from two Greek words: "Theos" (God) and "phos" (light). The originator of Theophostic Counseling, Ed Smith says, "These two terms describe God bringing forth illumination into a previously darkened area of one's mind. Theophostic counseling offers a new and revolutionary means of accomplishing what traditional approaches to therapy (failed to do)."

Theophostic therapists encourage children to rewrite their story from the point of abuse. If this type of therapy is used, it should only be with a trained counselor. Otherwise, a negative impact can result from this model of counseling. For instance, if a child is told that Jesus was right next to them when the abuse happened, they may wonder, "Was he watching me the whole time?"

Another effective method of counseling which can be done either by professional counselors or in pastoral counseling, is "Narrative Therapy." This model leads the child to rewrite his or her story from the point of counseling.

The Response of the Church

An appropriate starting-point for a discussion of the relationship between childhood abuse and the church is the central role attributed to the child in Christian thought. Jesus' love for children is clearly expressed in the New Testament. One of the only two times reported in Scripture of Jesus showing anger is in his response to the disciples attempting to keep the children from him. Jesus said, *"Let the children come."* They are the most vulnerable and powerless members of society. Christ identified them as both the least, in terms of their designated status in society, and greatest, in terms of their place in the Kingdom of God. In Matthew 18:5-6 we read a stern warning: *"And whoever welcomes a little child like this in my name welcomes me. But if anyone causes one of these little ones who believe in me to sin, it would be better for him to have a large millstone hung around his neck and to be drowned in the depths of the sea."* God is not silent when it comes to abuse.

Diane Lindberg, PhD., says, "I believe members of the Body of Christ who have been called to walk with survivors become the representatives of God to them. The reputation of God is at stake in our lives. We are called to live out in the seen, in flesh and blood what is true about who God is."

> *It has been said, "It takes a village to raise a child." I believe it takes a circle of many, a "Healing Circle," to nurture the healing of an abused child.*
>
> – Melodie Bissell

The child needs to see and understand unconditional agape love. In other words, we are to demonstrate the character of God over time, so that who we are reveals the truth about God to the survivor. As we provide pastoral care to the survivor within community, we are able to help the survivor or victim put down deep roots in the story of the Crucifixion. The child will begin to identify with the suffering servant, beginning to understand God's entrance into their suffering. As the church provides a safe place and a voice for the child, he or she will be able to grasp God as their refuge. Out of experience in the seen world they can better comprehend what is true in the unseen.

Francis T. Murphy, Presiding Justice (Retired) of the Appellate Division, states, "Children have neither power nor property. Voices other than their own must speak for them. If those voices are silent, then children who are victims of abuse may lean their heads against window panes and taste the bitter emptiness of violated childhoods."

Unfortunately these voices too often speak in silos and work in isolation of each other. The model of *The Healing Circle* provides an impetus to bring these voices together.

The Healing Circle Model

What it is:

The Healing Circle is a model for nurturing spiritual healing and wholeness in the life of an abused child. Its purpose in the church is to engage a child's community for the purpose of rebuilding walls of protection.

The church will be both incarnational and intentional in drawing the community that surrounds a victim together. The wise minister invites the seven pillars of Proverbs 9:1 – family, teachers, therapists, the church, friends, social systems and legal systems – to join together as a caring community around the victim. In a safe neutral environment, they "do" life together as a support to the child, family and therapist/counsellor.

The Healing Circle is committed to supporting the trained qualified professional counselor/therapist in his or her work with the child, while maintaining confidentiality. Together *The Healing Circle* will demonstrate grace and understanding. Through this model, the child will witness the strengthening and rebuilding of walls of protection, once again finding security.

The Healing Circle is not another program of the church, but rather a framework to draw together the family, friends and community of an abused child, with a desire to journey together to the place of healing and hope.

What *The Healing Circle* Will Do:

Child abuse whether physical, emotional or sexual – or neglect – can be devastating to a child. Once the abuse has been reported, the systems of the society kick in and it's easy to feel as though one is suddenly swept along in rushing, white waters. The Healing Circle will:

1. Help to navigate through these troubled waters
2. Embody the community of faith living incarnationally as they minister to a child and family during the turbulence.
3. Help to redeem the situation so that the child knows that God is not silent or distant but that He is taking the lead to rebuild walls of protection.

The Recommended Process for Implementation:

At the point that the church is notified or becomes aware of the abuse, through its mandate, it begins to provide pastoral care. A recommended process is as follows:

1. When the church is informed of the abuse, an opportunity arises to provide pastoral care
2. Recommend *The Healing Circle*
3. Begin slowly to build relationships with each group; ensuring confidentiality boundaries
4. Through pastoral care, help the child see how all these pillars are rebuilding walls of protection
5. Initiate opportunity to bring the helping parties together for coaching by the therapist

6. "Do life together" with the child

7. With care, help the child recognize and affirm commitment to rebuild walls of protection

The Seven Pillars of Proverbs 9:1

Family
Teachers
Therapist
Church
Friends
Social Systems
Legal Systems

***The Healing Circle* is Committed to:**

1. Engaging a child's community to model protection, support and care during the weeks, months and years after abuse has been revealed
2. Bathing the ministry in prayer
3. Maintaining confidentiality forever
4. Initiating supportive networks for both the child and family
5. Developing strong partnerships between professionals and caregivers

The Porn Factor

The naked human body is beautiful—wondrously beautiful. But when that vulnerable beauty is exposed to the public as a commodity offered for base consumption in the spirit of degradation, the angels must weep.

In-your-face smut

The word, "smut," is derived from a German word meaning, "dirt." It has nothing to do with the erotic sexuality of a healthy marriage.

Sexually explicit material has been around since cavemen experimented with drawings on their walls. Pornography is not new, neither does it have new material to work with. Humans and animals have the same number of parts they've always had. Females have breasts and vaginas. Males have penises. It's pretty basic.

What has changed is that people who liked to spend their time looking at drawings or photos of other people's parts, used to have to go looking for them. Suddenly, it's as though a tidal wave of smut has washed over society, showing up in practically every advertisement, television program, movie and internet porn mill. Sex sells in a society where people are preoccupied with looking at other people's parts.

We are becoming so accustomed to seeing images of naked and near-naked people that it's no longer an oddity. People are doing the 'full monty' on prime time television. The first time I saw people having actual intercourse as I surfed through the channels, I was stunned! And then came the "Naked News," where so-called news anchors systematically strip, totally naked, throughout the process of delivering a news story. How far are we going to allow this demeaning of humanity to infiltrate our society?

In today's media environment, children put in an average of 40 hours per week consuming its offerings. Just when parents think they've solved the problem by installing the latest filters, they get in the car for a pleasant family outing, only to subject the children all along the highway to steamy Ralph Lauren and Victoria Secret billboards.

Just as non-smokers are forced to breath the second-hand smoke of those who wish to use tobacco, those who do not choose to look at sexually explicit material are now sensually assaulted by second-hand smut at every turn. No one can live in North America in the twenty-first century without absorbing it. So much for democracy and the freedom of choice.

For those of us who do not choose to immerse our children and grandchildren in cultural trash, the task of raising them to be people of integrity and strong moral fiber has become daunting indeed: exhausting—discouraging—sometimes futile. The fathers and grandfathers who staggered in the muddy fields of the last great war to secure the future for us—their descendants—would weep in their graves to see the filthy success of the slimeball enemies of decency.

Another thing that has changed is the degree of perversion involved in the production of pornography. The producers know that addiction creates an insatiable appetite for more—but the problem is that they can't get any more raw material to work with. Humans aren't growing any more parts to feed the fascination. Women still just have two breasts and a vagina. Men haven't sprouted anything besides penises. Three parts for women – one part for men. Period. That's all the purveyors of pornography have to work with. Consequently, in order to change it up and maintain business momentum, the gazillion-dollar porn industry has had to pervert sexuality and normal bodily functions. (I apologize for the graphic nature of this paragraph and suggest that particularly sensitive readers skip the rest of it. I include this material only because it demonstrates a degree of the deterioration of our society.) So—they introduced oral, anal and genital sex between women and dogs, horses, pigs and all kinds of animals. Then came the bathroom games, including golden showers (urination), eating feces and painting them all over faces and bodies. Mutilation was sexualized with fish hooks through genitalia, fists in rectums and mousetraps on breasts. Champagne glasses were filled with ejaculate. Orgies featured oral and anal sex in groups. Torture and even murder were sexualized.[52]

But the worst—the worst—of all these atrocities was the sexualization of children for the consumption of individuals too sick to care about their own descent into hades.

---

52. Minnery, Tom (1986). Pornography; A Human Tragedy, Wheaton, Illinois, Tyndale House Publishers Inc., Dr. J. Dobson, p. 35.

The "pornographication[53]" of society

My new word. I wonder if it will make it into the dictionary next year along with "gazillion!" Pornographication is a good word, because nothing else adequately describes what is happening. We are changing from a culture characterized around the world as one of moral integrity and character to one so suffused by pornography at every turn that it has become part of our fiber.

With video games, the internet, television, music, magazines and movies increasingly dominating the lives of young people, media is becoming the most powerful source of influence in society. The age appropriate sectors of the media marketplace are supposedly segregated to protect children from seeing material that would interfere with their healthy development. However, entertainment ratings have become all but meaningless. All streams of media, even good old comic books, have become highly sexualized.

All sectors of entertainment compete with all other sectors because there is only so much time that people can give to entertainment. Thus, as cable television increases its sleaze factor, broadcast television does the same thing, dragging prime time television into the realm of adult entertainment.

Today's "PG-13" ratings equate to the "R" ratings of the early 1990s. For instance, "the 1994 movie *The Santa Clause* was rated PG, while its 2002 sequel, with an equivalent amount of profanity, sexual references and violence, was rated "G."[54]

---

53. Pornographication—"the conversion of an individual, group or society from normalcy, modesty and decency to acceptance of writings, pictures, films and behavior (usually considered obscene) intended primarily to arouse lustful sexual desire." (coined by D. R-L).
54. Reavill, Gil (2005). *Smut; A Sex Industry Insider (and Concerned Father) Says Enough is Enough*, London, England, Penguin Books, Ltd., p. 137.

When lines of tiny tot clothing are designed with adult sensuality in mind, it's time for a wake-up call.

This manipulation of the morality barometer has a direct bearing on the rise in child abuse incidents. By closing our eyes to the downward slide, we are contributing, not only to the pornographication of our society, but to the sexual abuse of our children.

The 1970s were the early days of video. Thinking themselves smart, thousands of people inserted the infamous Linda Lovelace tape cassette into their new video players and sat around to watch. Pornography is never smart. These days, that old video would be considered mild, but it was one of the building blocks of today's foundation of shame.

With video came the new boom years for pornography. The producer of *Deep Throat*, the Lovelace movie, invested $25,000.00 and earned more than $50 million in profits.[55] Videocasette recorders, phone sex services, home computers and pay television replaced the hard-to-duplicate 8-mm film, still photos developed in basement darkrooms and magazines delivered in brown paper wrappers—with live action in full technicolor. Millions of calls were made to dial-a-porn services.

As pornography began its overthrow of innocence, the world was awash in flower power and any voices that warned against the new moral liberties were not popular. The 1970 Presidential Commission on Obscenity and Pornography concluded that pornography was harmless, and that it even had potential therapeutic value.[56] When the social scientists, on whose

55. Minnery, Tom (1986). Pornography: A Human Tragedy, Wheaton, Illinois: Tyndale House Publishers p.53.
56. Minnery, Tom (1986). Pornography: A Human Tragedy, Wheaton, Illinois: Tyndale House Publishers p.115.

work this conclusion was based, told the world that porn was harmless, the floodgates opened and pornography quickly became increasingly explicit, degrading and violent.

A Public Health Hazard

By the 1980s, the effects on society were disproving the validity of the reports. Pornography had become unimaginably shocking to the uninitiated. C. Everett Koop was then Surgeon General of the United States. He warned that to ignore the evidence would be to make a conscious decision *not* to see pornography as a clear symptom of stress and disorder. He spoke of its "persistent presence" in four areas of human health:

- "First there is the field of sexual dysfunction. Pornography intervenes in normal sexual relationships and alters them in some way.
- "Second, one of the more disturbing pieces of information from our National Centre for Health statistics is the rising rate of suicide among young people. Recently, a number of these suicides were judged to be unintentional, the results of certain auto erotic behaviors in which soft-core pornographic materials apparently played a significant role.
- "Third, many women are justifiably concerned about so-called 'copy-cat' rapes. These are rapes that follow the pattern or 'story-line,' if you will, of a rape shown in a pornographic magazine or dramatized on videotape.
- "Finally...the effects upon individual children are profoundly harmful in physical, psychological and emotional terms. We suspect that the child who survives being used in this

> way may never again be able to function in normal human relationships. Tragically, a number of children do not even survive."[57]

At that point, while few studies had been done, speculation was rife that society was playing with a python.

Just before the Internet became common in homes, there was hope that children's advocates were beginning to rein in the child porn problem. At that time, it was thought that about 300 children were being victimized.[58]

But then the python wrapped its slimy cords around the world and began its slow squeeze against the breath of innocence.

With the advent of digital cameras and the Internet, photos of a new child being abused could suddenly go around the world in seconds. Computer hard drives can now store more video footage and images of child sexual abuse than any porn magazine library. With everything happening so fast, the unquenchable appetites of perverts for more and more new material is creating a demand for more and more shocking images. Thus, the age of children in the material is decreasing and the level of sadism depicted is increasing. Now the number of children being victimized as subjects of pornography is thought to be upwards of 100,000 worldwide.[59]

Deepening the victimization of the children used in this material, is the fact that once the images of their abuse is posted on the web, they are in permanent circulation. No matter whether the children are rescued or not, the theft of their privacy and innocence continues indefinitely. There is no end to it.

---

57. Minnery, Tom (1986). Pornography: A Human Tragedy, Wheaton, Illinois: Tyndale House Publishers p.107-108.
58. Margaret Sullivan, The Buffalo News, Oct. 21, 2007.
59. Ibid..

Rosalind Prober, president of Beyond Borders, when interviewed in the Canadian National Post about the arrest of a high-profile predator, said,

> "There is certainly an element of excitement that comes from the risk factor of sharing the pictures. Part of the sexual high comes from conning people, fooling people. There is some thrill seeking involved. It is a crime of impulse control, similar to addiction. It is also a case of networking on the Internet and finding a community and getting away with it for a bit and then getting sloppy. They're getting away with it so long they feel immune. It also shows how brazen these people are and how weak our system is for protecting children. It is really only the dumb ones that the police manage to catch, those so sexually obsessed that they take risks that expose them. The smartest and most sophisticated ones are very much out there."

Just because someone is not into *child* porn does not mean they won't molest a child. Any kind of pornography desensitizes a viewer to the humanity of the adults or children used in the images or videos. It's not about the heart or the mind: it's about the thighs, breasts, penises, vaginas and butts. Skin—anybody's skin—is just the surface of body parts to use for self-gratification.

More of my conversation with Matt:

D. When did you first get into pornography?

M. When I was a teenager, I went to work for a summer for my uncle in New York. I had my first car and I remember going into a corner store there and buying some novels that were very pornographic.

D. What led you to those books?

M. It was just curiosity at first and then sexual excitement and sexual gratification with masturbation. That kind of thing.

D. Did those novels contain pornographic material about children?

M. Not at first, but later on I did come across story lines that involved children, often in incestuous kinds of circumstances.

D. You've been talking about pornographic novels. When did you start into magazines?

M. About the same time. The novels were cheaper.

D. Did you find that as you got into porn, there was a desire for more and more explicit stuff?

M. Yes, although I never got into child pornography, other than what I came across by accident in those early novels.

D. I understand that you stopped using pornography for awhile. How did you get involved again?

M. With the internet. I saw some pop-ups and got curious and found there was tons of it.

D. How did you hide that from your wife?

M. Well, I just didn't go online when she was at home. I'd wait until she went out and then I'd get into it.

D. What would you say to someone who was just on the edge, was fooling around with pornography, hadn't touched a child yet, but was fantasizing about doing it? Knowing what you know now, what warning could you give a potential molester that could deter them from sexually interfering with a child?

M. It's a tough situation because, from a self-preservation standpoint, there's nowhere for the potential perpetrator to go without severe repercussions. If he hasn't touched a child yet, there hasn't been any law broken, but to go to anyone to discuss it, he would have to be very careful that it was the right person. But the reality is that if you do it, you're eventually going to get caught. Look at all these old priests, 70 and 80 years old who thought they'd gotten away with it all those years, but then the victims started to tell.

D. What if they've already molested a child?

If something has actually happened, people who know about it are bound by law to identify predators and predators have to come to the conclusion that they will have to accept the consequences. There's no way around that. They will have to pay the price, one way or another.

The thing is that if you've done something, in the grand scheme of things, you want to hope that you get caught on this side of eternity. If it doesn't come out until the other side of eternity, there's no chance to make anything right and you'll have to suffer in torment forever. You're done. There is no hope. Ever. You've got to get help. You've got to stop.

The good thing about facing the music, if there is a good part, is that they can stop themselves from hurting another child and they can have a second chance at eternity. For those who want to rebuild their lives and change, there's a good possibility that they may find a support group and the respect of mature Christians who will nurture them along in their battle.

I'm a living testament to that. I went from having a nice middle-class life with all the amenities; you know, a family, nice cars, big house, a half-decent business that kept us going for many years—to absolutely nothing. But I'm better now than I was with all that, because with a strong support group, I'm finally living an honest life.

I went to the first job I could find after getting out of prison—as a night watchman for a trucking company. I did well—got a raise far before I was supposed to get a raise—then they found out I'd been in prison and boom—they let me go. I was emotionally devastated.

If molesters turn themselves in, eventually they have to come to the realization that there is a certain segment of society that will never forgive them, no matter how well they try to do. There are those that already have and there are those who may eventually be able to.

But until something actually happens, there's still the chance of getting help. If I had known the pastor I have now, I could have talked to him.

D. Would you have?

M. Most likely not. In all honesty, probably not. But I could have because he's a guy you could reach out to who would make you accountable and get you help. And that's what you need. You can't just think, well I'm going to fix this, because you can't.

With all the therapy I've had now, I've found that there's a lot of secular garbage out there that just doesn't work. Undoubtedly it does help some people, but it's all about self-help and that doesn't always work because sometimes you need help beyond yourself. Secular fixes are all over the map. There are places that will tell you that pornography is a good thing, that it helps you get release—get into pornography so that you don't molest someone—but it's like—hello.

D. These are treatment places that are telling you this?

M. Well you know there are some who say, why don't you just go and get release with some porn instead of molesting a child.

That mind set is out there and it's perpetrated by the porn industry, because it's a multi-billion dollar industry and that's the bottom line. The buck. And it's not just sleazebags producing it. Media conglomerates that everyone thinks of as reputable are actually bankrolling these things. You listen to the lyrics on MTV. I'd name the sponsors but I don't want to get you sued. Everybody knows who they are anyway. This is the stuff kids are feeding on.

D. So you would not have gotten help without getting caught.

M. I don't think so.

While Matt was never into *child* pornography, the very nature of any kind of pornography gradually leads viewers into a desire for more and more explicit or unnatural material. Once whetted, the appetite for obscene images is insatiable. It's like a black hole that can never be filled. Had he not been found out, child pornography would no doubt have become part of his life.

Strangers in porn magazines don't need to be coaxed into the "mood." They don't require time "wasted" on foreplay. Porn is fast food for perverts.

Who the heck looks at child pornography?

Sitting alone in his tidy second-storey apartment, a thirty-something man listens to his latest CD and peers into his computer monitor, his freshly manicured hands directing the content on his screen. A screaming toddler is being raped, pleading for help. He watches, mesmerized, addicted to his revulsion. When that video ends, he prowls around the sites for even more graphic material. Who is this man and why is he on our planet?

David G. Heffler is a Lockport psychotherapist who is appointed by the courts to counsel child pornography offenders and has seen men from many different walks of life. In an article in the Buffalo News, he said that men who watch child pornography usually fall into one of two categories:

- Hard-core pedophiles and molesters who use child pornography to indulge their fantasies
- Men who start out looking at adult pornography but then "slide down a slippery slope" towards child pornography

> "Many men told me they started out looking at adult porn and never intended to look at children, but after looking at adult porn for a long time, they get bored. They want to try something different. They start looking at children. Then, they can't get enough of it."[60]

The usual responses these men give when asked why they look at child pornography include depression, drunkenness or their own issues arising from having been molested as children themselves.

A recent study by the U.S. Federal Bureau of Prisons[61] reported that 80 percent of the convicts studied who look at child pornography, acknowledged that they molested children—even if they were never charged with the crime.

The U.S. National Center for Missing and Exploited Children studied 1,713 people charged with possessing child pornography, 96 percent of whom were convicted. Almost all were male. Ninety-one percent were white. Forty-nine percent were sent to prison. Seventy-three percent had never been arrested for

60. Michel, Lou and Herbeck, Dan, *Confessions of a Child Porn Addict,* The Buffalo News, Oct. 21, 2007

61 Michel, Lou and Herbeck, Dan, *Confessions of a Child Porn Addict,* The Buffalo News, Oct. 21, 2007

a sexual offence. Eighty-three percent had images of children aged six to twelve and 19 percent had images of children under the age of three. Thirty-eight percent were married or were in stable relationships and 46 percent had access to minors at home or at work or through activities. Sixty-two percent had pictures of girls. Here's the worst—80 percent had images showing the sexual penetration of a child.

From statistics to real people

Behind every number added to a statistic, lies a real person.

Recently, a national newspaper printed an open letter from a man convicted and awaiting sentencing for viewing child pornography. The writer's purpose was to warn others what would happen to them if they, too, were discovered possessing child pornography.

He told of the sudden terror of having his home raided by 10 FBI agents who burst in and separated him and his innocent wife for full interrogation in separate bedrooms. Led away from his upscale home in handcuffs, he was further interrogated at the FBI centre and placed in a dingy cell with nothing but a cot and a toilet. Before being sent home to await a court appearance, he was called before a judge, instructed to retain a lawyer, photographed, fingerprinted and fitted with an electronic monitoring system for which he has to pay a $100.00 monthly rental fee.

When he called his boss to let him know what had happened, he lost his position, his income and his respect in the business world.

He spoke of the devastation of not being allowed to be alone with his grandchildren, of his nine o'clock curfew as he awaits his trial, of his loss of freedom to travel, of giving up his passport, being barred from voting and coaching children's sports, being rejected from his club memberships and unable to winter with his wife in his home in the south.

This man knows the likelihood that he faces prison time and it frightens him. The last sentence of his letter is a warning to readers that if they indulge in watching child pornography, they will regret not paying attention to his message.

Erotica or pornography?

There are those who quibble over the meaning of the word, pornography. They like to pass it off as harmless erotica. However, where erotica generally portrays sexual relations between consenting adults, pornography involves more than that. For my purposes, it refers to explicit or implied depictions of impersonal sexual activity where a child or a woman is portrayed as a one-dimentional, dehumanized object for sexual use or for displays of power of one individual over another.

A harmless pacifier?

The ordinary joe, who regularly picks up a couple of skin magazines at the news stand, loves to point out that it's better for men to look at pornography than to actually molest a child or act out some other kind of perversion.

Wrong, says Julian Sher, author of *One Child at a Time*.

> "Looking doesn't deter doing; study after study shows that 35 to 40 percent of those arrested for pornography possession are also hands-on abusers."[62]

62. Sher, Julian (2007). *One Child at a Time*, Random House Canada.

In order for there to be child pornography, someone has to be molested, and so the very act of indulging in the fantasies it evokes, contributes to its manufacture.

Increased exposure to the images leads to an addiction, increasing the desire of child porn addicts for increasingly stimulating smut. After feeding themselves with more and more graphic pictures, the point comes where pictures aren't enough and they want real interaction with a child. Evidence is overwhelming that there is a direct correlation between watching child pornography and eventually indulging in the sexual abuse of children.

Pornography desensitizes people to the pain suffered by the victims and glorifies the apparent pleasure of the assailant. Deviant activity is often falsely linked with pleasurable sexual responses, increasing the confusion factor in viewers.

When viewers watch children being sexually abused over and over again, their inhibitions gradually break down and they want to imitate what they have learned. They begin to think that because they're frequently witnessing this kind of behavior, it's widespread and more acceptable than they previously thought.

When they feed on images of perversion, regular sex becomes boring and unsatisfying. They hunger for something more adventurous, something less attainable, something with a titillating element of danger.

Virtual crack cocaine

According to Dr. James Dobson, Internet pornography is the new crack cocaine. The similarities between pornography and drug use are undeniable.

Like a drug, the watching of pornography results in the brain releasing endorphins, creating an intense feeling of euphoria, and creating a hunger for subsequent use. The "high" makes repeated viewing much more tempting ... and highly likely.

Continued use drives the need for stronger, more perverted images. What begins as viewing a picture has the potential to grow not only into an addiction, but into an encounter with a victim. Of course, not all porn users become child molesters and lose their homes and families, but of those that do, none imagined that to be a possibility when they first began viewing pornography..

Unlike drugs, however, pornography is available around the clock with no cost beyond an internet hookup and a computer.

Are you raising a child molester?

Every child molester was raised by someone. Sick people who molest children don't just suddenly appear, having stepped off the go-train from Mars. They are born into people groups, usually families, who are expected to guide them into healthy adulthood.

Parents and guardians have more of a shot at preventing the development of another predator than any politician, teacher or social worker. The home can be the germinating environment for either a healthy son or daughter—or a pedophile.

Force yourself to imagine walking down a long, concrete hall one day, pushing a buzzer at a door, entering a room lined with windowed stalls equipped with telephone receivers and seeing your son (or daughter) in an orange jumpsuit, on the other side of a window, waiting to talk to you via one of the receivers.

All your early hopes and early dreams for your child die right there as you are smacked hard by a smirking reality. Totally at the mercy of the guards and other inmates, in a world that doesn't care what kind of a big shot you are or what kind of a home he comes from, your child hangs his head on the other side of the glass, the embodiment of all the efforts, money and time you have, or have not, poured into him.

You stare at him, remembering all the violent, sex-laced video games you allowed him to play. A scene of life-like figures gang-raping a female on his monitor snaps across your mind. You remember the hours he spent alone at his computer while you zoned out in front of the television after a long day at the office. You remember the first time he found your stash of porn and how embarrassed you were at his questions.

You knew he didn't like himself very much, but you thought his aggressive behavior with younger children would fix itself. You remember the first time you discovered that he was logging on to porn sites and wish now that you had taken the time to figure out what to say to him about it. With shame, you remember the way you and your ex used to fight in front of him and the looks you saw on his face. You remember all those times you closed the door behind you, off to another social event while your child was left to his or her own devices.

Until faced with it in our own homes, we think of sex-offenders as anonymous faces splashed across the daily news. We suppose they were raised in some shapeless void from which they simply emerged as fully-ripened predators.

The reality is that child molesters are all born as sweet little babies. Their lives are blank slates upon which we as parents and guardians get to write. While some circumstances are beyond our control, the essential truth is that the more diligently we parent, the more details of our children's lives we address, the more accountability we require, the more positive goals and purposes we establish with our children, the more time we spend, the more we show them how important they are to us, the less likelihood we have of hearing the awful news one day, that they have sexually assaulted someone.

The less likelihood we have of having to walk down that long, lonely hallway.

As parents, we have a choice: we can bring cute little babies into the world and spend eighteen detailed years focussing on building enjoyable children who will contribute to life—or—we can bring cute little babies into the world and leave them to their own devices while we do our own thing and then spend the rest of our lives in misery, wishing we could redo those critical eighteen years.

Why do they do it???

While healthy humans are born with the propensity to engage in sexual activity, they're not born to be pedophiles or child molesters. Those desires are developed as a result of early experiences or interruptions in normal development.

Everyone needs to be touched and loved and paid attention to. As individuals mature, sexual satisfaction is added to the list of needs. During puberty, boys suddenly become totally preoccupied with sex. Their sex hormones increase fivefold within a two year period. Whatever sexual messages are delivered to them during that period are naturally going to have great significance. If they have normal interactions with females during that time, they are more likely to develop as heterosexuals.

On the other hand, if they are socially awkward and experience sexual arousal with the same sex or with someone considerably younger, it will be remembered as pleasurable and they may begin to seek out that source of arousal again and again, rather than changing the brain cues and seeking satisfaction from the normal, healthy source.

Women and pornography

Following the feminist revolution, it became trendy for females to claim interest in pornography and all things male. While the revolution gave a great boost to equal pay and opportunity movements, it had its downsides. Instead of standing their ground as authentic women with honest attitudes and values, many thought they had to deny their femininity and embrace traditional male attributes. They sold out and diminished the gender. They tried to become the gender they were fighting. Shock value was everything. What could be more shocking than to have a woman claim to enjoy watching others of their gender dehumanized, humiliated or perhaps portrayed as some kind of robotic, sexual gladiator?

While the number of female child sexual abusers is markedly lower than male abusers, researchers have documented evidence that women who expose themselves to pornography are just as likely as men to trivialize rape and to assume that a rape victim was probably promiscuous and wanted rough sex. Everything develops sexual overtones and so, when a child is abused, it's not such a big deal. The sexualization of a child is just part of the smutty mosaic of life.

Women who have bought into the acceptability of pornography in their lives need to take a close look at who they are and what kind of people they really want to be.

I would like to see the evolution of women go full cycle, right through to maximized womanhood. The feminist revolution hasn't gone far enough. It got sidetracked into a place it never had to go. Reaching the point of receiving equal pay for equal work did not require us to become stuck in some netherzone of unsatisfactory male cloning.

Yes, we may be more independent and better paid at this point in history, but we could have achieved the same thing by maintaining our femininity as real women who won't tolerate the advertising and pornography that demeans us and puts our children at risk.

The depths of hell

In doing the research for this chapter, I've touched down in the depths of hell. Even though I've taken the journey as a tourist rather than a citizen, I have no stomach for painting travelogue pictures. I don't want to take you there. In order to make my points here and there in the book, I've already had to be more explicit than I'd like to have been.

The hell of pornography in the 21st century is too dehumanizing to describe and I don't think I have to do it. Suffice it to say that when you have entertainment software companies developing life-like graphics that users can manipulate on the screen, undressing them, shackling and raping them, all to accompanying programed sounds, society has a problem. We need to wake up.

We can't think it's okay for a teenage boy to play these "games" for a couple of hours and then ride his bike around with the neighborhood children. His perversion-soaked mind is an assault waiting to happen.

My task

My task is not to expose every facet of modern pornography. My task is to show that it is linked to crimes against children and to be one small voice begging sane people not to indulge in it before they lose their humanity, their ability to have healthy relationships and risk turning their fantasies into criminal behavior which could not only land them in jail, but leave a trail of destroyed victims.

My task is to shake parents and say, "You have been given the privilege of shaping a life. Keep your mind strong and healthy so that you can raise a healthy child. Don't warp your child by allowing pornography anywhere near your home where he or she could come upon it. Recognize its incredible toxicity in the life of your family."

My message is that pornography is not just junk food for perverts—it's the main diet for people who molest our children. I'd like to see it wiped off the face of this planet.

We can make a huge change in this world by doing everything possible in our own corners of the world to eliminate it. I'm not naive. I know there will always be pornography. But maybe our efforts will stop one teenage boy from viewing it, who would otherwise have eventually molested one child. The whole world, for that one protected child, would be a different world.

The link between child sexual abuse and pornography

In January of 1989, Ted Bundy, America's notorious serial killer, engaged in his last television interview. He credited his progressive use of pornography with having led him to sexually mutilate and kill at least thirty women. He told James Dobson how, at the age of twelve, he had begun to indulge in the kind of "soft core" porn available at corner stores. He said,

> "Like an addiction, you keep craving something which is harder, harder, something which gives you a greater sense of excitement, until you reach the point where the pornography only goes so far. You reach that jumping-off point where you're beginning to wonder if maybe actually doing it would give you that which is beyond just reading about or looking at it."

The psychiatrist who was hired by Bundy's lawyers, later revealed that his first exposure to pornography came as a preschooler. His grandfather kept a stash hidden in their greenhouse and little Ted would sneak out there and look at the pictures.

In the interview, Bundy told how, just as his appetite for pornography was progressive, his murderous crimes began with peeping in windows and stalking women.

According to the latest research findings, use of pornography by sex offenders appears to be a major cause of sex crimes.

Clifford Olson, the worst serial killer Canada has ever known, violently murdered eleven children over nine months in 1980-1981. Two years prior to his killing spree, the police in Sydney, Nova Scotia, found pornographic pictures of young children in his luggage.

Story after story recounts the same progression of involvement with pornography where the photographs feed and legitimize deviant sexuality. With the mushrooming quantity of pornography over the past two decades, increased numbers of studies by social scientists have shown that such material has a negative effect on many who view it.

One of the best-known studies on the correlation between the availability of pornography and the rate of sexual assault was undertaken in Denmark. When the Copenhagen police and other researchers examined the data, they found clear evidence that violent sexual assaults had increased.

When South Australia loosened its constraints on pornography, the number of rapes rose sixfold.

Sociologists at the University of New Hampshire compared the sales of corner-store pornography with the crime rate in each state. They found a high correlation between sales and incidents of sexual assaults.

Pornography as child sexual abuse

People tend to think that premature sexualization of a child happens only with the actual touch of a perpetrator.

Not so. When a child is exposed to pornography, the experience can be so stimulating that it marks the brain. I remember baby-sitting when I was about twelve years old in a home with vastly different values than those of my parents. After the children were asleep, I pulled a movie magazine out of a rack and was totally shocked by the Frederick's of Hollywood lingerie ads. It was my first exposure to something so explicit and it affected me to the extent that I can still picture the ads clearly, 50 years after first seeing them.

If something like a lingerie ad affected me that much, imagine the effect on a child who gets into someone's hard-core porn stash or video library. Such children can become precociously aroused and begin acting out, perhaps with a younger sibling, thus perpetrating the sexual abuse.

Irresponsible parents who allow the possibility of such an introduction to pornography become complicit in the inappropriate sexualization of children. In the same way, when they "normalize" or display their own sexual behavior in the home, they are exposing their children to activity that the human brain is not meant to deal with at that stage of development. The result can be actual brain damage (see Chapter Eight, "It's All About the Brain") and inappropriate acting out.

The Internet - Trojan horse of the 20th Century

In the *Aeneid,* the poet Virgil tells of the fall of Troy in the 1100's. Having been unsuccessful in their efforts against Troy, the Greeks built a huge wooden horse and left it outside the walls of Troy. They then pretended to sail away, defeated, in their ships. After a Greek prisoner convinced them that the horse was sacred and would bring the protection of the gods, the Trojans decided to pull the giant wooden horse into their city. Little did they know that Odysseus and other warriors were hidden in the body of the horse. That night, as Troy slept, the Greeks crept out of the belly of the horse and opened the city gates for the rest of the warriors who had returned from a nearby island.

While the Internet has revolutionized society in wonderful ways, the enemies in its underbelly have invaded our homes from within. It has become a unique enabler of child-porn offenders. The more technically astute they become, the more images become available to them.

By creating new ways of offending, the internet has spawned destructive addictions and criminal obsessions.

There is a tidal wave of new molesters being groomed to abuse children from what they've seen on the internet and other forms of pornography. Never before in the history of the earth has such graphic material been available to pervert the minds of young teens. The first wave of their initial offences will be disastrous to all levels of society; but if they continue to offend after their primary incarcerations, the cost to society will be so overwhelming that we will break under the burden. The good news is that there are some wonderful people out there working day and night to decrease the size of the wave.

No matter how tirelessly these unsung heroes work, there are always going to be predators who slip through the cracks and molest our children.

Heroes of the day

Having fingered internet pornography as one of the most critical factors in the development of a predator, I believe it makes the most sense to dry up the flood of smut. However, draining the Internet of child pornography would seem to be an impossible task. But with modern day heroes like Jim Gamble, there is hope.

Jim Gamble is the C.E.O. of the Child Exploitation and Online Protection Centre (CEOP), the United Kingdom's centralized agency for fighting sexual child abuse. I first read about him in Julian Sher's book, *One Child at a Time* and, for the first time in a long time, I caught a glimmer of hope that 'the good guys are gonna win.'

The motto of CEOP is, "Making Every Child Matter Everywhere." Launched in the U.K. in 2006 as a centralized clearing house run by law enforcement, it fights child abuse with a coalition of specialized disciplines from the computer industry, child protection groups, credit card companies, social agencies, educators and a variety of industries. The different specialties all bring their expertise to the table, providing the widest perspective possible from which to hunt down and catch predators and rescue children from abusive situations. CEOP's international tentacles reach around the world, plucking out people who profit from child trafficking and catching travellers who use child prostitutes in third-world countries.

Jim Gamble has come all the way around the block. He started his work with one goal in mind—catching and arresting offenders. Then his vision widened to save the children who are the subjects of child pornography. Now his focus is on stopping pornographers from making the videos or taking the pictures *before* a child is abused.

Working with Jim Gamble in CEOP is Joe Sullivan, a brilliant forensic behavior analyst blessed with an abundance of common sense. Having departed from the wild west philosophy of rounding 'em up and throwing away the key, Joe insists on understanding the offender. He believes that by studying their triggers and their behavior, there is more probability of stopping them. With the numbers of men who admit to fantasizing about having sex with a child, it makes so much more sense to help them deal with their thoughts before they commit a crime, than to wait until a child has been victimized and then try to make some sense out of the situation with jails and courts.

Having tried other methods, Jim Gamble recognized Joe Sullivan's wisdom in striving to understand who the predators are and how they think. Julian Sher, in his book, *One Child a Time*, quoted Gamble as saying,

> "Let's better understand the nature of the person who commits the crime and then let's see if we can police this environment in a wholly different way....If we're going to divert people from this, we're not going to do it by continually arresting people. We recognize that some offenders are more dangerous than others, but for many of the others we need to have a crime reduction strategy, a diversion strategy."[63]

Gamble began to take a different tack with his news conferences. He began to appeal to potential predators with less aggression and more reason. He would say, "If you're sitting at home tonight, listening to the radio or watching TV, or reading this article, and you have inappropriate feelings towards children, for goodness sake go and seek help now. Go to your doctor, go to someone you can trust...divert yourself from this path. Otherwise, in this day and age, more than likely you're going to destroy your life and that of your family. Because we will catch you."[64] He firmly believed that the behavior of pedophiles could be influenced and moderated by fear of being caught.

---

63. Sher, Julian (2007). *One Child at a Time,* Random House Canada. p. 60

64. Ibid.

Internet deterrents

Another hero in the internet porn war is Detective Sergeant Paul Gillespie, who served the Toronto Police Services for over 27 years. In 2003, Gillespie was running Canada's largest child exploitation unit. Having seized three million pornographic photos of children the previous year[65], he was overwhelmed with the horrible truth that "the bad guys were winning." It seemed impossible to get on top of the incredibly sophisticated encryption and filtering techniques they were using. It was as if the police would plug one hole in the dike and a leak would spring up in a totally inaccessible location.

Thumb drives, wireless drives, cell phone cameras and portable personal devices are all providing new avenues for the traders and producers of child pornography to send and store their collections. The task of finding a child who is a subject of this material is like searching for a particular grain of sand in a desert.

In total frustration, Gillespie hammered off an e-mail to Bill Gates, blaming Microsoft for providing a venue for the explosion of child abuse images on the internet. He basically said: Your technology helped create this mess; help us clean it up.[66] He never expected an answer—but he got one.

Gates read the message and contacted Frank Clegg, then the chairman of Microsoft Canada. That led to a meeting of some of the top Microsoft experts with Paul Gillespie and the police. Gillespie decided that the best way to demonstrate the problem was to show the computer team a handful of the images the police have to deal with every day.

---

65. Sher, Julian (2007). *One Child at a Time,* Random House Canada. p. 64.
66. Ibid, p. 65..

Frank Battison, the senior team leader for the project, described the experience. "He warns us there are five pictures; turn your heads if you want. It was horrific. Absolutely horrific. I saw one, looked at number two. And I just turned away. Didn't want to see anything else. And to this day I still have those two burned in my head. I want to get rid of them, and I don't know how. But it certainly inspires you to do what you can to eradicate these problems."[67]

When Battison took a look at the archaic resources available to the police for fighting the battle, he was stunned. He said, "The police were being asked to catch pedophiles, and the task would be equivalent to sending somebody out in a rowboat in the middle of an ocean and saying, 'Catch some fish.' And the only fish that they're really able to catch are the ones that jump in the boat!"[68]

The upshot of the meetings between Microsoft and the Toronto police was a decision to cooperate in the building of a database that could compile and connect police data to find links to pedophiles and abused children within the millions of graphics and bits of information. The database was called the Child Exploitation Tracking System (CETS). Microsoft committed to invest several millions of dollars to work towards Paul Gillespie's dream of building CETS into an integrated, international tool available to every law enforcement agency for tracking predators and finding victimized children.

When the police found and rescued the first child through CETS, it was so thrilling that it set Microsoft on the path of investing millions more and enlarging its scope beyond what anyone had hoped was possible. Gillespie was encouraged beyond bounds.

67. Ibid p. 65..
68.Ibid p. 65..

"We're taking back the Internet. The bad guys have long used it as their communication tool. Well it's our turn. And we'll see who's left standing."[69]

Accepting responsibility

The message of raw pornography is regurgitated by the general media's negative depiction of women and the rendering of sexual relationships to base usage of flesh. Until the message of the media is changed, legislation is going to have little effect on how people view physical bodies.

In order to protect the most vulnerable members of society, we have to move away from viewing sexuality as a commodity and re-render it to its place in healthy relationships. That involves the necessity of the media working to protect the innocence of childhood and finding more creative ways to sell products than through billboard-sized pictures of body parts. Titillation and disregard for the value of women and children have no place in the entertainment industry or in the marketing of goods and services.

When children are inundated with images of sex and violence day after day on television, in comics and in video games, the messages of pornography become more reasonable and acceptable to them. They become *pornographied*.

The media must begin to monitor itself. It has made aggression edgy and chic. When translated from the brain of a viewer into real-life, there can be dreadful repercussions—and there's no scroll of the cast of characters at the end.

Healing society starts with us individually in our own homes,

69. Sher, Julian (2007). *One Child at a Time,* Random House Canada p. 68.

teaching our children to love and be loved, teaching them wholesome values so that they will make wholesome choices. Taking time to communicate healthy, selfless love to the little ones we bring into the world is the turning point for healing our world.

Getting Help

For those addicted to pornography who sincerely want help, the idea of having people find out, particularly in a church setting, can be prohibitive. Many addicts are high profile, upstanding citizens of the community with a lot to lose. The probability of rejection and ostracism is very real and too great to risk.

While it would be wonderful to think that confession and a request for help would be met with understanding and willingness to assist in healing, recovery and restoration, the reality is that it's difficult to find effective treatment in the church or community. Thankfully, help is available from the same source pornography addicts feed their addictions – the internet. In the same way they hide their dark activities, they can hide the process of restoration.

A few links to freedom:

http://www.freedombeginshere.org

http://xxxchurch.com/gethelp/

http://x3watch.com/

http:/en.wikipedia.org/wiki/XXXchurch.com

http://www.no-porn.com/breaking.html

http://www.purelifeministries.org/index.cfm

It's all About the Brain

I do not write as some lofty observer, telling victims to get over themselves and spinning clicheéd philosophies. Not at all. I have experienced the agony of a mother of an abused child. I have known the grooming of a predator. I have felt the shock of betrayal. I have struggled through restoration in situations of unbelievable brokenness. I have sat, stunned, listening to horrifying news. I have been there.

So—what do I do with all this? What do people do when life circumstances conspire against their desires to live good, healthy lives?

As I see it, even when chunks of our lives have been stolen from us and chewed up in a grinder, we have choices. It all happens between our ears and in our hearts—in our brains.

No matter how life or any individual may treat us, we get to choose how to respond.

I admit that at this age, having experienced all that life has presented to me, positive, productive responses have gotten easier and easier to master. There's a certain 'toughening' that happens with repeated opportunities to be strengthened.

Victim or victor?

There are those who see themselves as pieces of flotsam and jetsam, tossed here and there with no personal control. There is a sense in which they're sometimes right. There are some things over which we don't have control.

But even though no one chooses to be abused, abuse cannot be a cop-out for life. Life holds so much beyond victimization. We must never let any kind of abuse define us. We are more than results of somebody's sin or sickness. We are individuals who can walk through the abuse into the light of freedom.

It angers me to see victims further victimized by people who enlarge on the situation, thereby encouraging a martyr complex that, unless broken, could trap them for life.

A person allowed to live behind dark "Woe is Me" walls will never enjoy the stimulation of rising above circumstances.

Hatred is another trap, settling itself like a black bag over the head of the victim, tied at the knees to prevent forward movement.

Sometimes those surrounding an abused child will heighten the effect of the abuse by filling the mind of the victim with their own hatred for the offender. Little do they realize that the offender isn't the one who suffers from the negative programming, but that they are further victimizing the child, trapping him or her in their own emotional bondage.

In order to regain life after abuse, the mind of the victim has to be given permission to let go of every negative emotion tied to the abuser and let God and the law do the job of dealing with the perpetrator.

The mind of a victim needs to be encouraged to heal in a positive, encouraging environment and slowly begin to rebuild towards the future. The past is past. That's why it's called the past. It's over. There is no future in the past.

Damaging and healing the brain

There is plenty of evidence surfacing to suggest that the stress of child molestation can cause actual brain damage in some individuals – but that the damage may be reversible.

In recent years, counselors and psychologists have discovered that emotional, sexual, and physical abuse can have physiological impacts on victims that may exceed the damage originally inflicted by the abuse.

Psychologist Dr. Joe Troiani, Director of Behavioral Health Programs for the Will County Health Department in Joliet, Illinois, in speaking about the mind-body connection, said:

> "Trauma will have an impact on the brain, probably especially a child's brain. Trauma research has shown that because of biopsychosocial aspects, the body still feels it even though it's past the trauma. We are integrated in terms of our minds and our bodies.... You cannot have good physical health without good mental health. Abuse, even emotional abuse, tends to have a physical impact."

New research affirms that mind-body connection. An article by Benedict Carey in the N.Y. Times, February 23, 2009, deals with the common knowledge in the psychiatric community that "children who are abused or neglected run a high risk of developing mental problems later in life – from anxiety and depression to substance abuse and suicice." The question is whether the abuse causes biological changes that increase the liklihood of these problems.

Cary goes on to say, "In a study ... published Sunday in the journal Nature Neuroscience, researchers in Montreal report that people who were abused or neglected as children showed genetic alterations that likely made them more biologically sensitive to stress.

This can lead to physiological problems as adults struggle to deal with the challenges of life. In normal adults, certain receptors in the brain detect cortisol, a stress hormone, and help clear it from the brain. However, adults who were abused as children had as many as 40 percent fewer receptors, and their cortisol was not cleared from their brains as effectively.

Physical changes seen in the brain decades after child abuse may be just one of the long-term consequences of abuse. Troiani said other physical manifestations of child abuse seen in adults can be problems with the cardiovascular system, digestive system, headaches, back pain, problems sleeping, and other behavior difficulties.

Childhood is a unique period of progressive development on all levels of maturation. The brain is influenced by early experience. Study after study shows that child abuse experiences may cause delays or deficits in the ability of some children to develop in an age-appropriate manner. If scientists can determine how abuse harms the brain, it may help in efforts to learn about how to heal broken lives.

Children are especially at risk of having damage done to their brains, because their growing minds don't know what to do with the terror and frustration of abuse and so they internalize it, thus increasing the stress on their entire systems. It is so sad that the terror is often inflicted on the child by a family member or someone they trust.

In the October, 2007, edition of the Scientific American.com, Scott Lilienfeld and Kelly Lambert reported on the work of neuroscientist Bruce McEwen's group at Rockefeller University.[70] They found that chronic stress alters neuronal complexity in three key areas: the medial prefrontal cortex (involved in working memory and executive function), the hippocampus (involved in learning, memory and emotional processing) and the amygdala (involved in fear and intense emotions). Dysfunction of the amygdala in abuse-related situations may lead to problems modulating emotion.[71]

McEwan found that chronic stress reduces length and branching of dendrites in the brain's medial prefrontal cortex by about 20 percent. The result seems to be an impaired ability to shift attention in the process of learning new skills. Also affected may be the ability to distinguish reality from fiction and an increase in vigilance and suspiciousness.

According to Dr. Victor Carrion, child psychiatrist at Lucile Packard Children's Hospital, this means that,

> "there may be some real neurological reasons for the impulsivity, agitation, hyper-vigilance and avoidance behaviors that children with untreated post-traumatic stress disorders often exhibit."[72]

70. Lilienfeld, Scott O. and Lambert, Kelly (Oct. 2007). Brain Stains, Scientific American.
71. Bremner, Dr. J. Douglas (2007). The Lasting Effects of Psychological Trauma on Memory and the Hippocampus, Law and Psychiatry, p. 7.
72. Science Daily, July 30, 2007. News release issued by Stanford University Medical Centre.

This may mean that some children wrongly diagnosed with attention-deficit hyperactivity disorder (ADHD) may in fact be having trouble concentrating and doing certain tasks as a result of post-traumatic stress disorders resulting from sexual abuse.

The hippocampus is particularly sensitive to stress. While reduction in its volume revealed other symptoms of the stress caused by abuse such as memory lapses, anxiety and an inability to control emotional outbursts,

> "exciting recent research has shown that the hippocampus has the capacity to regenerate neurons."[73]

Once viewed as genetically programmed, the brain is now known to have plasticity and can be changed with life experiences! This fact, accompanied by results of studies, holds out hope that positive experiences may actually reverse some of the damage!

There is a great deal of work being done on brain studies that demonstrate the importance of "growing" the brain in positive directions.

Forgetting—in the sense of "setting aside"

The conclusion of the Lilienfeld and Lambert report was that "forgetting" (setting aside - refusing to be defined by) traumatic events may offer the best chance for regaining mental health.

I believe that conclusion to be extremely important in guiding victims of sexual abuse into a place of healing.

For some, the idea of "forgetting" about abuse that has happened

73. Bremner, Dr. J. Douglas (2007). The Lasting Effects of Psychological Trauma on Memory and the Hippocampus, Law and Psychiatry, p. 3.

is totally unacceptable because it would not only minimize its importance, but risk repeated vulnerability with regard to the perpetrator. It would be thought to be almost blasphemous in the face of such injustice and trauma.

Quite the contrary. By protecting, holding on to the memory and erecting it as a defining life event, those surrounding an abused child may prevent healing.

Who Switched Off My Brain?

In her fascinating book, *Who Switched Off My Brain?*, South African brain specialist Dr. Caroline Leaf presents astounding information on the brain, which is supported by current information. One critical piece of knowledge is the understanding of how one can "grow the brain at will."

Dr. Leaf contends that correct, positive thinking will "grow" the brain by forming new connections, new neural pathways. Even as people age, they can continue to increase their intelligence as long as the input is positive and healthy.

Thus it would appear that refusing to dwell on the toxic thoughts of past injustices or abuse, but rather striving to dwell on positive, healthy topics can restore some damaged brain functioning through growth of new connectors.

Bad memories hurt us every time they are accessed. Allowing toxic thoughts to wander through one's mind, unchecked, will eventually make one sick. Through exchanging those memories for positive, healthy thoughts, the brain can literally be "detoxed."

I found it fascinating to learn about the "anatomy" of a thought—how thoughts are conceived, develop and take root in our psyche.[74] What was particularly enlightening, was the realization that thoughts are not just intangibles that waft in and out of our heads. They actually have chemical substance and, as such, need to be controlled.

Dr. Leaf contends that the primary means of healing toxic thoughts, emotions and bodies is by consciously controlling one's thought life.

> "Research shows that an enriched environment of thinking positive, healthy thoughts can lead to significant structural changes in the brain's cortex in only four days. Frequent and challenging (positive) learning experiences build intelligence in a relatively short amount of time."[75]

Dr. Leaf's own research for her PhD demonstrated that:

> "potential can be increased 35 percent to 75 percent if people are taught how to understand their brains and to think properly."[76]

My point here is that we have the choice of allowing nasty, negative thoughts to keep us in a toxic quagmire, unable to move ahead—or taking control of our thoughts, replacing negative ones with positive ones, enabling us to walk out of the past into our future.

Dr. Norman Vincent Peale, in his books on the power of positive thinking, tapped into the resources available to us in overcoming

---

74. Leaf , Dr. Caroline (2007). Who Switched Off My Brain?, Switch on Your Brain, Rivonia, South Africa, p. 13-44.
75. Leaf , Dr. Caroline (2007). Who Switched Off My Brain?, Switch on Your Brain, Rivonia, South Africa, p. 114-115.
76. Leaf , Dr. Caroline (2007). Who Switched Off My Brain?, Switch on Your Brain, Rivonia, South Africa, p. 114.

the circumstances of our lives. It was he who identified the "law of attraction," so popularized in the trendy 2007 book, *The Secret*.

While it has an element of truth, Peale's law of attraction is quickly revealed to be flawed with the ridiculous suggestion that the universe is at our beck and call. It's just flashy marketing of the old concept of wishful thinking now distilled down into the latest plastic trend which isn't really much of a "secret."

On an individual level, however, his concept of the power of positive thinking can be helpful when applied to the ability of an individual to reprogram his or her brain. Within the constraints of circumstances over which we have control, the application of this concept can be life changing.

Nineteenth-century philosopher and psychologist, William James, said,

> "The greatest discovery of my generation is that human beings can alter their lives by altering their attitudes of mind."

The Bible, in 2 Corinthians 10:5 says,

> "...we take captive every thought to make it obedient to Christ"

meaning that we have the ability to control our thought life, rather than allowing it to run rampant with negative thoughts that pull us down. We can turn a toxic thought into a healthy, positive one at will.

Circumstances don't need to dictate our quality of life, as revealed by the responses of different individuals in comparative life circumstances. Napoleon, after apparently having enjoyed all that life has to offer, in his final exile to St. Helena, claimed that he had never had six happy days in his life. We've all read stories of incredibly wealthy people who have relied on drugs and alcohol to mask their misery; but of others, like blind, deaf and dumb Helen Keller who claimed to find life so beautiful. It's all in the attitude, the way they think about life – what they do with their thoughts.

The heart as a mini-brain

Until recently, when people spoke of the heart as the centre of their emotions, we never really thought they meant the "heart." After all, everybody knows that the heart is a pump. As it turns out, however, the heart is much more than that. It actually acts like a mini-brain. It has its own independent nervous system with at least 40,000 neurons, as many as are found in various subcortical centres of the brain. It acts like a "checking station" for all the emotions generated by the flow of chemicals from thoughts.[77]

Science is discovering that the heart's brain is a real "intelligent force" behind intuitive thoughts and feelings.

In *The Spiritual Brain,*[78] neuroscientist Mario Beauregard and journalist Denyse O'Leary present a case for the physiological existence of the soul, or heart of man. There's a wealth of new information on how the brain relates to this entire topic. If they are right, we may have to consider a whole new field of knowledge,

---

77. Leaf , Dr. Caroline (2007). Who Switched Off My Brain?, Switch on Your Brain, Rivonia, South Africa, p. 71.
78. Beauregard, M and O'Leary, D. (2007). *The Spiritual Brain*, A Neuroscientist's Case for the Existence of the Soul, HarperOne, San Francisco, CA.

> "where neuroscience, philosophy, and secular/spiritual cultural wars are unavoidably intermingled."[79]

According to brain specialist Dr. Caroline Leaf, it is dangerous to the physical condition of your heart if you do not forgive. In her book, *Who Switched Off My Brain*, she lists some of the dangers of toxic emotions to the heart:

- Hypertension (high blood pressure)
- Angina—chest pain and spasms of the heart tissue (heartache)
- Coronary artery disease—hardening of the arteries causing narrowing. This can be triggered by anger.
- Strokes or cerebrovascular insufficiency—the clogging of blood vessels so brain tissue becomes starved.
- Aneurysm—ballooning or swelling of the artery or rupturing of blood vessels. This can also be triggered by anger.

Positive affirmations

After my son's revelations of abuse, I instinctively believed that if we could reprogram his negative thoughts about himself through positive affirmations, it would be helpful. I had received a list of positive affirmations based on God's promises in the Bible and I began to read them to him every night before he went to sleep. At the time, they were helpful for both of us. We needed something concrete to anchor us.

79. Publisher's Weekly, June 11, 2007.

The truth is that training ourselves to think positively can turn our brains around.

Positive affirmations are tools to use in controlling thoughts. For every negative thought you have about yourself, you can construct a short sentence to counteract it. That's an affirmation. For example, if you feel that no one likes you, you can change the thought to, "People like me," or if negative thoughts of being ugly torment you, you might replace the thoughts with, "I am a beautiful person." The more you repeat these to yourself, the more acceptable they become to your brain and the less power the negative thoughts will have.

The more ingrained the negative thoughts are, the longer it will take to reprogram our minds. It may take several months of repeating an affirmation over several times a day before it overpowers the negative belief and takes root.

The trick is to recognize the negative thought as soon as it enters the mind, grab hold of it, reject it and replace it with the positive affirmation.

Whether or not you believe the affirmation has nothing to do with the process. For instance, if you are feeling as though no one loves you, you can say, "I am lovable" without having a shred of belief in the truth of the statement. However, as you continue to repeat it, over an over again, the feelings that match will gradually emerge.

Activation of the will

Getting control of one's mind requires discipline and repetition of effort. The natural inclinations of our minds are not always going to lead to the best outcomes.

For instance, when someone does us wrong, the natural inclination is to build a wall of resentment, anger – or whatever negative emotion. However, as we have seen, toxic thoughts do not serve us well. Besides being counterproductive, they have been proven to be unhealthy.

But toxic thoughts are not always easily routed. Things like forgiveness can be almost impossible for some people in some circumstances to accomplish. It's almost as though the pain of something like betrayal or abuse is so deep that covering it with bitterness feels like protection. But toxic responses to life bear nothing but toxic fruit. The only way to overcome unproductive natural inclinations is by taking charge of the brain by forcing ourselves to push past natural inclinations to the place of mental and emotional healing.

Pushing past bitterness

Forgiveness is a very tough issue when it comes to matters of child abuse. However, with Dr. Caroline Leaf's contention[80] that it is dangerous to the physical condition of your heart if you do not forgive, it's obviously important on more than one level. Nevertheless, the pain of a parent or of a victim can be so deep that the mere mention of the word is like a slap across the face, an unwelcome intrusion into the sacred place of bitterness.

But because unforgiveness does more damage to the unforgiver than it does to the unforgiven, somehow it has to be activated with authenticity.

Most often, forgiveness must begin as an act of the will. Emotions like resentment, bitterness or hatred are the cerebral stew from within which forgiveness must find a way to surface. The only

80. Leaf , Dr. Caroline (2007). Who Switched Off My Brain?, Switch on Your Brain, Rivonia, South Africa,

attention our emotions can have in situations like this is our determination not to give in to them. They have the potential of destroying us. Every thought has to be taken captive and brought into submission to the will of God (2 Corinthians 10:5).

Forgiveness is a decision – the culmination of a process of thoughts – not an emotion. When we make the conscious decision to forgive, purely as an act of the will, the emotions of *feeling* forgiveness will eventually follow. As the determination to forgive grows, it gradually displaces the negative emotions with the sweet savor of peace.

In my own experience, true forgiveness was activated only by a supernatural switch – my dependency on God – to channel His forgiveness through me to the offender. That is how I let go. That's the only way I was able to cleanse my brain from the deadly toxins of bitterness. I was unable to do it on my own.

We can try and try and try to forgive through applying our head knowledge to the needy areas of our lives, but until we come to the place where we actually allow the Holy Spirit to do the forgiving through us, there cannot be total rest. In this case, it's not all about the brain – it's about *submission* of the brain to the Holy Spirit.

I learned a lot through my friend Anne's efforts to forgive. She has consented to tell her story.

Anne's story of forgiveness

Ted and I have a daughter and two sons. I never wanted much more out of life than a wonderful, warm family. My own Dad and I had never been close, and when I met Ted's family, I really felt that I had come home. Although I dearly love Ted, sometimes I wonder who I really fell in love with most – him or his family!

When our first little baby girl, Laura, came along, I was overwhelmed with the wonder of life and the thrill of motherhood. One by one, as our two sons, Danny and Brian, came along, that thrill was renewed and I felt that there was no limit to my love for these children.

Everything seemed to go along so well for a while. Ted's parents were wonderful with the children, and I poured myself enthusiastically into every area of their precious lives. I never minded getting up in the middle of the night to tend crying babies. I enjoyed the challenges of helping each one to learn things like cooperation and responsibility. I loved watching the development of these little people and spent hours reading stories to them, taking them to the park for rides on the swings and teaching them silly songs. They were so much fun. I really loved being a mom.

I was a very careful mother. I always made sure that the kids had balanced meals and clean clothes. Laura's curls were always brushed and shining and they were never left anywhere by themselves. Ted and I never went out unless we knew that the baby-sitter was absolutely trustworthy and was someone whom the children would enjoy. Whenever we were away overnight, we left them with Ted's parents. Sometimes I used to think that I was overly protective, but with so many dreadful things in the newspapers, I just didn't feel that I could be careful enough. I couldn't bear the thought of any one of these little ones being victimized in any way.

As the years went by, all three of the children seemed to be developing beautifully – for the most part. They were all healthy and bright. There was just one thing that nagged at my mind.

Danny had always been a very well coordinated little fellow. Of all the children, he had always been the happiest and best liked.

However, by the time he was about four or five, he began to have problems with his coordination. The doctors were unable to find anything and dismissed the whole thing as rapid growth. But there was more. For some reason, Danny began to favor the company of younger children, and the children his own age began to reject him. More than once, he came home crying that the kids had called him names. Smiles became a rare thing for Danny and his once healthy carriage became slumped and defeatist. Constant stomachaches led to a diagnosis of an ulcer. What was wrong? Why would a young boy have an ulcer?

Night after night, year after year, I spent hours trying to encourage Danny and build his self-confidence. Night after night, he cried himself to sleep. Why? He was always such a good little boy. It broke my heart to see the way the other kids rejected him, but what could I do?

About this time, Ted and I began to have some major struggles with our relationship. Through it all, we began to look beyond ourselves for purpose in our lives and found Christ. It wasn't long before Laura, Danny and Brian, now ten, nine and seven respectively, also accepted Jesus as their Savior, and we were suddenly living a very different lifestyle, centered on Christ and His teachings.

Naturally, we were very excited about what we had found and were most anxious for Ted's parents and my parents to come into a personal relationship with Jesus as well. My parents were so convinced about the reality of Jesus by seeing the change in our lives that they accepted almost right away, and it was wonderful for me to come into a close relationship with them for the first time in my life.

Ted's parents, however, were a totally different story. They thought that we had gone right off the deep end and made no pretense about how they felt about us. We began to feel very uncomfortable with them and desperately desired their salvation. For a long time we prayed for them with no visible results. If anything, their hearts seemed to harden with the passing of time.

During this time we tried to maintain as normal a relationship with them as possible because we felt that it was important for the children to maintain a close relationship with their grandparents. Ted's dad had always seemed to have a special soft spot for Danny, and it seemed to us that should help little Dan with his self confidence. Naturally, whenever the children were invited to their home, we allowed them to go.

Occasionally, when I would go into Danny's room at night to tuck him in and pray with him, the words "molestation" and "suicide" would flash into my mind. Instantly, I would push the thoughts out of my mind because the very idea was so foreign and frightening. Little did I know that the Holy Spirit was trying to warn me with the gift of discernment of spirits about the battle we were in.

By the time Dan got into high school, his personality had suffered damage and he was experiencing real difficulties with relationships. Laura and Brian, on the other hand, were carefree, popular teenagers. What was the difference? They had all been raised in the same home with, we thought, the same determining environmental factors.

Where was God? Ted and I had struggled for years with Danny, and yet the situation just seemed to deteriorate. Why were our prayers for him not being answered? Why had our beautiful little baby boy grown into this emotionally conflicted teenager who cried out desperately for love but was unable to receive or give even a simple hug?

Finally, in desperation, Ted and I prayed that God would reveal the *root* of Danny's problem.

A few days later, I went out to get the mail and found the *Last Days Ministries* newsletter in the box. On the cover was a lovely little house with a winding path leading up to the door. It was all done in faux needlepoint and looked so cosy. Also in faux needlepoint was the title, "Incest, the Family Problem."

I remember so well feeling a great compassion for anyone involved in this, but feeling at the same time great relief that was one problem we would never have to face. I casually left the magazine on the counter and forgot all about it.

That night, Danny was particularly disturbed and I sent Ted in to talk with him, as the situation was beyond me. Ted was in Danny's room for about an hour.

When he finally came out and sat across the table from me, his words "My father has been molesting Danny for years," did not even penetrate my mind. They just sort of sat there outside of us, on a wall of disbelief, too horrendous to absorb. We went to bed and went to sleep. Even the next day they did not seem real.

However, by that evening, it was like the freezing coming out of a tooth. The hollow, bottomless ache set in. We were in agony of soul. It was like a death of a very dearly loved one. It was the recognition of the death of Danny's sweet innocence, the murder of his childhood, the rape of his trust. All of our efforts to keep Danny safe and protected from the ugly things of life had been undermined and sabotaged by Ted's own father. What evil would make a man betray his own son—through defiling his son's son? Does perverse selfishness actually know those depths?

"God – why?" I silently screamed over and over out of my torment. "How could You let this happen to my precious son? I prayed and prayed for him. Don't You care? Aren't You there? I did the very best job I could with Danny. I tried my best to be a good parent. Where were You? Why didn't You do Your part?"

Finally, in the stillness of my emptiness, the answer came: "Just as I allowed the death of My Son for your salvation, I allowed this to happen to your son for the salvation of Ted's dad. But just as My Son rose victorious in the resurrection, so your son too, will be restored."

I wept. I knew He wasn't comparing my son to Jesus – just giving me some insight into how He planned to redeem this horrendous, devastating situation.

That afternoon, I picked Danny up from school early as he had an eye appointment. Over a coke at *McDonald's*, he told me what he had told his dad. He had read the article on incest that had come the day before, and the wise and godly advice in it had given him the courage to tell us what he had concealed for so many years.

All of this time he had felt the weight of family unity to be on his little shoulders. He knew that if he told, Grandpa would be in trouble and so he just bore the situation until he was big enough to say no. By the time he finally told us, he had not allowed his grandfather to touch him for over a year. He had accomplished his goal of keeping his family together, but at an awful price.

Ted and I really didn't know what to do. We had never had any experience with courts or the law. It was the eighties and no one was talking about abuse – much less incest. We didn't have a frame of reference. I was afraid that if we involved the police, Danny would have been put in the awful position of having to testify and send the grandfather he loved (in spite of everything) to prison. I didn't want this thing to take one more chunk out of my son's life. If I had known then what I know now, I would absolutely have involved the police because, for one thing, it's the law that abuse has to be reported and for another thing, Danny needed to feel that justice was served on his behalf – and for another thing, Ted's dad should have been punished.

However, out of the rubble of our confusion, the only thing Ted and I could think of was that as Christians, we had to forgive his dad. However, we also knew that he had to be confronted with our knowledge of the situation and it was not just to be swept under the rug. My natural inclination was to scratch his eyes out, but wanting to find the very best way of handling it for my son, I struggled to find God's way.

Thus, I went to a Christian bookstore and bought a Bible and some relevant books which I felt would be helpful for him. Because of the relationship, Ted could not face his dad, so I phoned him and he agreed to meet me at a restaurant.

At first he denied everything, attempting to make his grandson out to be a liar on top of everything else he had done to him. But finally he confessed to everything and agreed to read the books. I told him that until he got himself right with God, he would not be welcome in our home and that our children would not be in his home. The strength that God gave me in that meeting was awesome.

That was Thursday. On Saturday morning at eight a.m., there was a knock at our door. It was Ted's dad. He was broken. He had read Andrew Murray's book on forgiveness and wanted us to know that he had asked God to forgive him. He wanted to accept Christ and followed Ted in a prayer of salvation.

And so, after years of praying for this man, he was finally saved. How could I hate someone who was now a child of God? Suddenly, everything was okay for him. With one little prayer, his life had been made right.

But what about us? What about the shambles this man had made of our home? Who would give my son his childhood back? School relationships were still the same for Danny. Attitudes and defense mechanisms learned over the hard years were not going to go away with a poof and a couple of "I'm sorry" words. What about Ted and the pain of his father's duplicity. What about me? Could I ever smile again? Would laughter ever ring spontaneously from my lips? What about Laura and Brian and their heritage of such unspeakable sin? Was that all going to go away with one easy little prayer?

Day after day the tormenting thoughts of hatred taunted me and my efforts to forgive. Day after day Ted and I tried to help Danny to pick up the broken pieces of his life. Day after day, night after night, we prayed for Danny's promised restoration.

Step by step, month by month, healing progressed. Almost right away we saw a change in his posture. Other things, like coordination and relationships were slower, but the progress was visible and so encouraging.

Had Ted's dad taken a strong hold on the Christian faith and spoken forth his allegiance to Christ to the rest of Ted's family, we might have been able to overcome our pain a little faster. However, fear of their reaction to his acceptance of the very thing for which he had condemned us for so many years kept him quiet. The distinct possibility that his declaration of faith had simply been another manipulation to get him out of trouble was something we didn't even want to think about. I knew God had given him a very costly chance – but the ultimate choice was his.

And then he was stricken with a terminal illness. How I battled my thoughts of hatred and tried to act out my words of forgiveness by sending him cheery little notes each day and trying to act loving and natural whenever we saw him.

"God, I know that I have to forgive. But I can't do it. You have to do it through me. You know I've tried. It's too hard. How much do You expect of me? I'm just not that strong. "

Day by day, his life was eaten away by the disease. Finally, one night as I was leaving his hospital bedside, I turned back to look at him and he said, "Sorry for all your trials and tribulations. "

"That's okay." I smiled and walked out – empty.

He died two days later.

As I sat beside Ted in the memorial service, the minister talked of heaven and I contemplated the thought of his dad being there. I had always thought of heaven as a place inhabited by vague, misty, perfect people. But now, envisioning Ted's dad there ruined that ideal. To me, he wasn't a perfect person and he didn't fit in my heaven. Furthermore, if that's where he was, then I didn't want to go there. The relief of not having him on the same planet as me was still fresh and exhilarating. I was free from his presence and didn't even want to think about ever having to be in the same place as him ever again.

Sitting there, I prayed, "Lord, this is wrong to feel this way. Help me through this one." Suddenly I realized that Ted's dad fit perfectly in heaven. He had asked God for forgiveness of his sin here on earth and so he was just the same as everybody else in heaven. They were all just forgiven sinners, and that's what qualified them to live eternally with Jesus.

Taken somewhat aback at this fresh revelation, I contemplated my own inabilities to live a perfect life and realized that I was no more or less qualified to dwell in heaven than Ted's dad. I, too, was an undeserving sinner whose only redeeming justification was the fact that I, too, had been forgiven.

For the first time, I saw myself on equal footing with Ted's dad. I was no better than he. It made me appreciate Jesus in a new way. To suffer and die for perfect people and then to prepare a beautiful eternal home for those perfect people was one thing – but to invite sinners like us to live with Him in that lovely place forever was quite something else.

Now, when I envision Ted's dad in heaven, I still see him as the same old person. The difference is that he's wearing a spotless white robe, washed clean through the blood of Jesus. All of that evil has been washed away through forgiveness.

Finally, I truly feel that I have accomplished the forgiveness that I so long struggled to give, but I know that I could easily slide back into unforgiveness if I were to begin once again concentrating on myself and accepting Satan's negative suggestions. Maybe a real test of forgiveness is asking oneself if he or she is comfortable with the thought of sharing heaven with the offender.

Although Anne has forgiven her father-in-law, she speaks occasionally about her struggle with recurring feelings of bitterness. She still works at replacing the negative feelings with compassion and love because the wounding was so deep, but there is no evidence of the bitterness she refuses to allow to take root in her mind. Her key to maintaining this state of forgiveness is walking moment by moment in conscious knowledge of the presence and strength of the Holy Spirit.

With the passing of time, Ted and Anne have seen the faithfulness of God in restoring their son and bringing him into a deep relationship with Jesus.

It often takes time for the emotions to heal, even though forgiveness has been planted in our brains. Even with an external, physical wound, unless there is a miracle, healing takes place in stages. The wound bleeds for a while and acute pain is generally present. Then, as the pain becomes a dull throbbing, moisture may ooze for awhile. Eventually a scab forms, then hardens, and eventually drops off when the healing is complete underneath. The same principles are generally present with forgiveness. As we forgive, the pain becomes less and less acute.

Forgiveness can be one of the toughest things in the whole universe. In my own life, I felt very guilty about my difficulty with it until, one day following a time of prayer, God showed me that, for Him, forgiveness was so hard that He had to send His Son to die for us. That is what the cross was all about.

Forgiveness. It is the pivotal point of the whole universe. Mark 11:25 confirms that if we don't forgive others, God cannot forgive us.

The battlefield of the brain

I believe that much of the spiritual warfare waged against us happens in the mind through negative suggestions from demonic realms. While much of what we battle originates with our own human natures, there is a dark side to the realm of the spirit where evil forces actively pursue our destruction. Anyone who doubts this needs to read the Bible where they will find that one-third of the ministry of Jesus dealt with aspects of spiritual warfare and the enemy of our souls.

While this is not a book devoted to the topic of spiritual warfare, no discussion of the function of the brain in relation to matters of child sexual abuse would be complete without warning of the care that must be taken to live our lives in accordance with the Spirit of God. Overcoming the dark thoughts that try to impose themselves in our minds can only be fully accomplished through replacing them with the promises, precepts and principles of Scripture.

Healthy brain – healthy body

If we hold unforgiveness in our minds, we can fall prey to all kinds of diseases. According to Dr. S. I. McMillin in *None of These Diseases*, "Carnal emotions produce stress-which some authorities are now questioning as being the cause of all disease." Unforgiveness is the root of tremendous stress in all sorts of relationships.

Forgiving God

Although God's provision for the forgiveness of man has been and will always be the greatest theme of the universe, yet there are times when man's greatest difficulty is in directing his or her thought processes to the place of forgiving God, believing Him to be the source of their woes.

A famous broadcaster experienced a very difficult loss of one of his family. He blamed God for the death and spent the rest of his life ridiculing Christians and lashing out against God. As far as I know, he died as bitterly as he lived, unaware of the true source of his sorrow.

It is not uncommon when we experience heartache of many kinds to question, "Why God?" What appears right and good and logical in our eyes may look totally different from God's perspective because He is all-knowing. We have to trust that in His great love for us, He truly is working all things together for our good even though it may not look that way. The more we experience the presence of God in our lives through times of struggle, the more we can trust Him when something devastating happens to us.

God knows how much we hurt and He aches in seeing us hurt. It is all right to express our grief to Him. Our anger and feelings of loss or betrayal are no secret to Him. He is patient with us as we work through our feelings. He is the One who sustains us through it all.

But in the end, there is a place of sweet unity where, as an act of the will, we can say, "Nevertheless, not my will, but Thy will be done." At that place, we find willingness to absorb the hurts that God has allowed in our lives. At that place there is rest.

Refusal to enter into that rest means self-destruction through bitterness and unforgiveness. If those who have a hard time finding peace and forgiveness continue to ask God for it, it will come.

Jesus never said that we had to feel that the other person was in the right in order to forgive him. He just said to forgive. In the end, it doesn't even really matter who was right and who was wrong. All that really matters is us as forgivers.

In forgiveness, everyone wins. In unforgiveness, everyone loses.

Renewing the mind

The healing of memories and emotions, soul healing, or renewing of the mind, as some prefer to call it, is not a matter of probing all through the past, dredging up every distasteful incident. It is a matter of allowing the Holy Spirit to reveal and heal painful areas in the brain which block us from going on with our lives.

Renewing of the mind often comes through a conscious willingness to enter into a painful memory and allowing Jesus to give deeper understanding of the circumstances and forgiveness. With Peter, Jesus took him right through the three stages of his guilt and healed him step by step. This sort of healing can be likened to peeling the layers of an onion.

When we speak of Jesus as our healer, it is often just as the healer of our bodies, and we forget that we were created in the image of God, as triune beings. Jesus wants us to be whole: body, mind and spirit. He came not only to bring us salvation and physical healing, but to *"bind up the brokenhearted and set the captives free – and to set at liberty them that are bruised"* (Luke 4:18).

As we grow into chronological adulthood, we all bear the scars on our souls of wounds that have been inflicted through the years, whether through abuse or other painful circumstances. In renewing our minds, God reveals understanding and restores us – sometimes through situations, sometimes through meditation, sometimes through His written Word or a special word of assurance to our hearts – and sometimes through dreams.

Jean is a lovely friend who endured a traumatic situation a few years ago. She was not a Christian at the time and was confused and deeply wounded. Through it all, she came to know Christ and found in Him the real purpose for her life. However, the deep pain of the memories remained.

One night, after soaking her pillow with her tears, the Lord gave Jean a gentle dream of healing. When she arose, she wrote it down and has given me permission to share it in the hopes that it may bring healing to the minds of others as it did to hers.

Memree

"She's all I have, " the child said, clutching her battered, dirty doll closer. Several lumps of cotton wadding protruded further through the gaping holes in its dirty body as she squeezed it to her. One leg dangled grotesquely, the stitches which once held it in place having broken and rotted away after years of misuse. Fascinated yet fearful, the child moved back into the shadow of the alleyway. Her shoes seemed about to speak as the soles flapped loosely open at each step she took. Two dirty toes could be seen peering out from the torn canvas top.

The man remained still and silent. His face was kind and his eyes took in every detail of the child's obvious poverty. He remembered how she had followed him for weeks, slipping noiselessly from doorway to doorway, supposing herself to be unnoticed.

The doll was always with her, as dirty and uncared for as the child. Its face was stained and torn and most of its hair had been lost. A n old baby's dress adorned its mutilated form, and from the way it lay now, caught up in the child's arms, he could see a very large hole in its body.

The child was about eight years old, with eyes that searched constantly to detect the slightest hint of danger. "More like an animal than a child, " he thought, remembering how she had stalked him week after week. Fearful, poised, ready to run at his slightest movement, she stood still in the shadows. The man showed no annoyance. He simply remained still.

She called him "the man with the shining face," since she didn't know his real name. Each day she would watch for him, and he was always there. He drew her like a magnet, and yet her fear caused her to keep her distance. He had surprised her one day by turning and smiling his gentle smile. In her panic she had fled, but the next day there she was again.

"Does your doll have a name?" he asked quietly.

She studied his face and pulled one dirty shoe across the other. "I call her 'Memree.'"

"What an unusual name. Why do you call her that?"

Deciding to answer his question, the child informed him that one day she had overheard her mother saying that a dear friend was very unhappy and seemed to be losing her memory – or "memree" – as the child pronounced it. She had sat and pondered this strange statement.

What could the lady be losing that would make her so unhappy?

The only thing that would really grieve her, the child decided, was if she were to lose her doll. And so she had called it Memree ever since. She watched his face for a reaction.

He did not laugh at her, but nodded his head. "How long have you had Memree?" he asked.

"For just about ever. She's always with me. I don't ever remember not having Memree, not ever." Warming to his interest, she said, "Are you sure you won't hurt her if I let you hold her?" That was the question that had driven her back to where she now stood. He had asked if he might see her doll.

"I promise," he said gravely. "Maybe you would like to sit beside me and make sure that I hold her properly."

Silently she sat beside him, the doll half behind her back.

"You see," said the man, "I can fix her up for you; that is, if you'll allow me the pleasure."

The child did not understand his words, but she felt his sincerity.

"Are you a doctor?" she asked.

He smiled. "Yes, I have been called that."

She pulled Memree forward and the leg fell silently to the ground. The child bent down and her eyes filled with tears. "Can you mend this, too?"

"Oh, yes." He held the doll as tenderly as he would have held a newborn baby.

"Will it hurt her?" asked the child.

"No," he said, "but I'm going to need your help. I have to know what happened to her if I am to mend her. This mark on her face-how did she get that?"

"Oh, " said the child, "that happened when she was thrown out of the window when I was fighting with my brother."

The man put his hand on the place. When he removed his hand, the mark was gone.

The child looked from the doll's face to the man's face and back again. "How did you do that?" she asked in wonder.

"You told me what happened to her and then I was able to mend her because I knew how she was hurt."

Excitedly she began to tell him about the various injuries until her eyes fell on the large hole in the body. She alone must take full responsibility for that. The other injuries had involved her brothers and sisters, but this one was different.

"Maybe he won't see it, " she thought, and reaching our her hand, she took Memree back into her own arms. Pulling the dress down over the guilty place, she said she had to go now.

It was a week before she ventured back again. He was there.

Somehow she had known he would be. She sat down without a word and placed Memree in his lap. "I think she needs more help," she said, her eyes pleading with his. She had been tormented by the thought of the hidden wound all week. Part of her wanted Memree healed, but part of her was sad about what she had done. "I didn't mean it," she said. She looked down at her feet which were gently swinging back and forth.

"How did it happen?" he asked.

She looked up, her eyes full of tears. "She got burned. I shouldn't have done it. My mother told me, but I did it anyway. When I saw the burn, I tried to cut it out so no one would know. She showed him the ugly place. "It's right near her heart," she sobbed.

"I can mend hearts, too," he said softly, placing his other hand on the doll. The ugly hole was gone when he took his hand away.

Her eyes shone, this time with joy. Every mark was gone from Memree's face and body. She almost seemed to be smiling in her lifeless way. "She's beautiful," said the child reverently, and clutching her precious possession tightly, she slipped from the seat and ran towards home. Halfway there, she stopped. Her mother might ask her who had done this beautiful work. "I forgot to ask him his name, " she thought aloud. "Never mind. I'll ask him next time. He's always there.

Exactly one year later, the Lord gave Jean a second dream about Memree, challenging her to see that the memory was just hidden rather than released, even though she had thought that she had really given that part of her past over to Him. Now, according to His timing, she was ready for the next step of healing – for full release.

This time, the child had grown into a young lady who still loved Memree but longed for the elegance of womanhood.

She looked lovingly at Memree and said, "I can't take you with me. You are part of what I was, but not part of what I am." She laid the doll down and covered her over gently and then went out to the spot where she always met the man with the shining face.

"You came today to talk to me about your tomorrows. You are concerned about being ready for the days ahead. Memree helped you to come to that place of understanding. Without her, you would not be what you are today. "

"Little one," he said, "I could tell you many things, but that would only confuse you. Let's talk about us. Your life has become caught up with mine. You are the harmony to a beautiful melody that I am going to play through your life. My life and yours gently blending, always in time, always in tune. Sometimes the bass notes of sadness will be woven into the music, but they will be there to make the high notes of joy ring ever more clearly. The prelude has already been written and played with you and Memree and me, but before I can begin the next part of the music, I need all of you. Although you no longer carry Memree in your arms, you still carry her in your heart. Will you let me take care of her for you?"

She felt as though her heart was being ripped from her body. She hadn't realized how much Memree meant to her, even now. Through the intense pain of the moment, she could feel the touch of his hands, still holding hers. "Why can't I let her go?" she wept.

"Because you are trying too hard and you are trying alone. Why don't you ask me to take her for you." And then they were at her house, looking at the covered doll. With tears blinding her eyes, she picked Memree up and laid her in the man's arms for the third time – but this time it was forever.

Exhausted, she slept. When she awoke, she was in his arms. The pain was gone, and a new quietness lapped about her and over her like gentle wavelets. They were warm and deeply satisfying.

With all of our talk of freedom, democracy and choice, no matter which part of the world we call home – no matter our circumstances or heritage – the extent of our freedom lies along the boundaries we have established in our minds.

Boundaries like unforgiveness, bitterness and hatred keep people walled off from life behind great thick walls of self-preservation. Gradually, the walls grow toxic mould that poisons from within. While it may seem scary to allow the walls to be disintegrated from the light of the love of Jesus, allowing them to crumble is the only route to freedom.

In the search for freedom, whether from the standpoint of a victim, the loved one of a victim or a perpetrator seeking to be rid of perverted temptations, each of us needs to have our minds renewed. We need a new mind-set that values things like kindness, integrity, mentoring, patience, consideration, concern for others, gratitude, generosity, forgiveness, compassion, empathy, respect, restorative justice and wisdom.

Freedom to be all we were created to be means letting go of the negativity, despair and hopelessness that try to impose themselves upon us and replacing them with the positive affirmations and promises of God, battling skillfully against the spiritual warfare that seeks to destroy us..

In the process of renewal, we need to be highly conscious of those who do not espouse the same values and be well educated as to their tactics, while not allowing ourselves to become entrapped in their dark worlds.

When the Worst That can Happen – Has Already Happened

When the worst that can happen has already happened and your child has been sexually abused, the challenge is in finding the best path to healing for the child in the face of dealing with your own agony. That's not easy.

Providing an atmosphere conducive to healing

The angst of those surrounding the child is understandably so raw that the abused child often picks up hatred or bitterness and ends up carrying a heavier burden than she or he had to begin with. For that reason, it is critical for a parent to examine his or her own feelings, recognize areas that need healing and not transmit those to the child who needs to recover.

When Ed and Lois Smart's beautiful daughter, Elizabeth, was abducted and kept from them for long months, she returned to a home that understood the principles of building together towards healing, enabling them to emerge from the pain together, rather than becoming entrapped by martyrdom and unforgiveness. From all appearances, it would seem that they are all recovering amazingly well from incredible trauma.

If the caregiver is successful in finding effective counseling for the child, it can be tremendously helpful. For a young victim to work through the issues early in life, rather than having to drag them through every relationship, is so important.

Healthy and unhealthy coping skills

If an abused child does not have an opportunity to come to terms with issues, he or she can go through life applying the same coping skills used to get through the abuse, to all the relationships that follow. For instance, if a child develops manipulative skills or becomes good at lying or deception to hide the abuse, success in future relationships will be denied if those characteristics remain. It's not possible to have any kind of meaningful relationship with a deceptive person who lies. There's no guarantee that anything he or she says is true. When trust is broken, the relationship dies.

During the time of the abuse, it may have been very helpful to be able to lie or manipulate, but coping skills used to adapt to abusive situations are not skills required in healthy relationships. When applied in a non-abusive relationship, they introduce toxic elements that can destroy something that could otherwise have been beautiful.

Issues that have arisen during or as a result of abuse need to be identified and rectified before healthy relationships are possible.

The myths of isolation

When something like the sexual abuse of a child is discovered in a family, it is so traumatic that the tendency is to feel that the situation is unique, that no one else could possibly have gone through such agonizing circumstances.

The natural response is to try to wrap the child in cotton batting to protect him or her from suffering any more pain. However, if a family communicates this mind-set of isolationism to a victim, it will make him or her feel even more out of the loop of humanity and as though he or she is the only one with any problems.

The reality is that pain and suffering are part of the human condition. If present stats are showing that more than one out of every two girls suffer sexual abuse and at least one out of every three boys, the reality is obviously higher because of the number of unreported cases. It would seem that abuse victims are in the majority of the population.

It's important for a survivor to be aware of these numbers—not in any way to minimize the importance of their trauma—but to instill in them a connection to the pain of other people and recognition of the fact that they're not abnormal. It's all about the development of compassion and self-acceptance.

Willingness to be open

While it might be easier at the time to try to sweep things under the carpet as though they didn't exist, the lumps and bumps will eventually begin to show. It's better by far to tackle healing head-on. Initially it will be more painful than letting things rest, but wounds have to be opened and cleaned out. Otherwise, a victim keeps giving the rest of his or her life to the perpetrator.

When victims begin to understand the way the abuse has affected their lives, they can begin to respond differently to life. When they can stop trying to hide what happened and allow it to surface in normal conversation, the pain begins to dissipate and the abuse gradually loses its hold over the victim, allowing him or her to get on with life. It becomes recognized as a reality of one's past, but is no longer an issue that affects other relationships. The absence of pain is the sign of real healing.

Being released from the pain of a memory and forgetting about it are two different things. Telling a child to try to "forget about it" is like telling them to try to forget what school was like. The abuse is a part of their reality. However, the reality of memory does not have to carry pain with it forever. The pain can dissipate. The memory will remain.

The challenge for parents and guardians is to find a way to lead a child through the pain filled memory to the place of peace and healing. Encouraging a child to maintain walls of hatred ties them in debilitating bondage to the abuser. Letting go of the hatred and bitterness is the only way to freedom from pain.

I am realizing in writing this chapter, that much of what I have learned comes from the mistakes I made along the way. While I wanted to do everything right and have everything turn out well when I discovered that one of my children had been abused, I wasn't entirely successful. There was so much that I didn't understand about the process of justice and healing.

While I have come to value personal transparency, in those years, I was in mama bear mode and wanted to do all I could to protect my child from further destruction to his life. I wanted him to feel that others regarded him as normal. I thought that if they knew he had been abused, it would be more difficult for him. And so I tried to handle matters on my own, rather than involve the court system. Little did I understand that I was denying my child the opportunity of seeing justice done.

Helping loved ones who have been abused

The goal of every parent of an abused child is to eliminate the effects of the abuse and get the child back into the healthy groove of normalcy.

That journey can be one of the most frustrating, painful and sometimes frightening challenges imaginable. Every fiber of the parent's being is bent on fixing the broken pieces of the precious child. But an abused child is not like a broken vase that can just be reassembled and glued together. No one can see all the pieces and even if they could, children can't be controlled to the extent that a parent can do all the fixing themselves.

The choice of whether to be healed or to remain broken depends largely on the response of the child. Oprah Winfrey made the trip through her abuse to a place where she is able to help others to an incredible degree. She has used her pain to spur her on to conquer life rather than allowing it to conquer her. But then we read of shattered lives that have ended in suicide; people who have jumped off bridges, taken pills or slit their wrists in a final statement that the journey was just too hard.

Then there is the great throng of those in between the two extremes—people who have survived and have recovered to greater and lesser degrees. If we can believe the latest findings, that throng is composed of more than half of the women on this planet and at least a third of the men.

How does one "fix" a broken child?

In helping a child to recover, the first hurdle is to recognize the fact that a vase will never be the same as it was before it was broken. Some pieces are lost forever. Others may be so shattered that it's futile to even think of trying to use them in a repaired vase. No one can "fix" a broken child any more than they can make a broken vase new again.

But who says that the pieces of a broken vase have to be made into a vase again? Beautiful mosaics could never be crafted into works of art without broken pieces.

In preparing the raw materials for his work, the artisan takes a hammer and shatters something that began as something else—a dish, a vase or even a mirror. Without the shattering, there would be no raw material. He knows what he's doing. The pieces don't understand that there is a purpose in being broken – but the artisan can already envision the finished product within his plan.

Before some children can heal, they need to feel their brokenness and be given the freedom to express all the rage, shame, grief, aloneness, betrayal, confusion, fear, anxiety and hatred that they have repressed for perhaps a very long time. They need to be able to uncover it, hold it up to the light to see what it looks like and then decide what to do with it. A parent who doesn't understand that need could prevent the deep healing needed.

A parent who does understand that need can be an invaluable channel of healing. A parent who has the wisdom to find the beauty in the brokenness and then help the child to love and appreciate that part of himself or herself is a priceless resource for the child, because a broken piece of a mosaic will always be a piece of that mosaic. It has even more value as a mosaic than as a vase. The process of healing involves embracing the brokenness.

What does that mean – "finding the beauty in brokenness?" What would that look like?

Finding the beauty in brokenness means appreciating the broken piece for what it brings to the whole mosaic and teaching the child how his or her pain can be turned around to help another person on his or her road to healing. One of the most obvious points of light is called "empathy," the ability to come alongside another person and say, "You're not alone. I understand you. I am where you are. We are both valuable pieces of this mosaic. Without us, something special would be missing in this world." Another point of light is called, "compassion," the ability to feel and understand reality with a depth impossible to reach without it.

Real healing doesn't require a return to the original condition. It means submitting one's self to the hands of the artisan and becoming comfortable with the new mosaic – seeing its beauty. The new mosaic includes the reality of the abuse and accepts it as part of the whole design of life—both the smooth and the broken pieces. No one ever forgets abuse. The memory doesn't go away, but with the process of healing, the pain gradually fades.

It's important to understand that the new mosaic will include the entire spectrum of human emotions. Anger, impatience and resentments will surface from time to time, but they'll become less and less toxic. The new mosaic will include changes in perceptions and attitudes, new ways of seeing the world and relationships.

From Angela to angel

Towards the end of her award-winning documentary, "Searching for Angela Shelton," Angela Shelton met another woman by the name of Angela Shelton who tracks sexual predators and lives in the same town as the filmmaker's father, who sexually abused her and her step-siblings while they were children. On *Larry King Live*, Angela told about being abused by three different people in her childhood and being date-raped at the age of 15. Through making her film, she found other abuse survivors who taught her about forgiveness, faith and the power of the human spirit. Now, as a voice for survivors of trauma, Angela started the Angela Shelton Foundation, whose purpose is to inspire and empower survivors of abuse to heal and lead joyful lives. Her film "started a grassroots movement of survivors and humanitarian organizations around the world who are breaking the silence about the epidemic of abuse."[81] The details of her work can be found on her website, *angelashelton.com*.

Purpose in pain

If a child is allowed to wallow in his or her own misery, without being directed to see the pain of others and focus on how they can help to alleviate their suffering, he or she will risk growing into a bitter, self-absorbed martyr.

81. angelashelton.com

It can be a great relief for a wounded young person to feel as though they have something to contribute to the human condition of others. A parent who understands the importance of guiding a survivor of abuse to become a compassionate soul who can contribute to life will be a wonderful help to finding the path to true healing for that child.

This doesn't mean saying, "Come on, snap out if it. Suck it up and get your mind on how you can help other people." Not at all. It may be some time before a wounded child is ready to exercise some compassion for others and reach out beyond himself or herself.

It's a strange thing, but the more we pamper our children through the hard patches in life, the less kind we are to them. The best parenting involves lovingly empathizing with the suffering of our children so that they will know how deeply we connect with them, but gradually pulling them through to the place where they can use their own pain as a tool to help others.

When they can see that their own problems have purpose in life, as raw material for helping others, everything changes. The powerlessness they felt as abuse victims becomes strength as it is put to work helping others. As they feel this strength begin to emerge, they begin to see a new truth about themselves—that they have a voice and are not helpless.

The bottom line is that every rotten deal thrown at us in life can somehow be turned around to become a treasure. That process of discovery can be a whole lot easier if we are surrounded by wise people who understand that principle. For instance, when John Walsh's little son, Adam, was murdered, John's refusal to allow his little boy's death to be in vain resulted in enormous benefit to society and gave the Walsh family a surety that Adam's life was not lived and left for nothing.

Getting there

What I have just written is probably the most important thing I have to say in this whole book—but getting an abuse victim to the point of reaching out as a whole and compassionate person is not an easy road. Dealing with a child who has been molested can be one of the most frustrating and painful processes imaginable.

Confusion is one of the most damaging residues of abuse. Life has been turned upside-down. Trust has been replaced with distrust. Innocence has been capsized by perversion.

Life is confusing enough for any child, just learning and growing with normal circumstances, but when something like abuse is thrown into the mix, the confusion can be overwhelming. Finding the way through a tangle of unexpected, unplanned, unnatural challenges can throw a child into such tremendous imbalance that everything around him or her seems off kilter.

The frustration will often lead a survivor to take out his or her pain on the parent or caregiver. There can be so much rage and pain inside that the survivor doesn't even know who he or she is mad at. All persons in positions of control or authority can blur into one faceless blob of blame.

It's bewildering for a parent to pour love and support into a child and be rewarded with accusations, hateful glances and rejection. The parent is already going through his or her own pain concerning the situation, but to be suddenly treated like the enemy by the precious child he or she is striving to help, is almost unbearable.

The thing for parents to understand is that they are not the real targets. For the duration of the abuse, the child was unable to express his or her real feelings about the situation. Once disclosure or freedom came, the constraints were gone, but the old emotions of betrayal, hatred, indignity, pain, grief, aloneness, misunderstanding, helplessness and worthlessness remained. All that poison has to come out and whoever is closest or safest is going to get it sprayed all over them. This could take a short time...or a long time.

Because of the depth of betrayal, the child may expect betrayal from others and will test over and over and over again for trust. He or she will work hard to find things that they think they can't trust about the parent or caregiver and then say, "Aha. I thought so." If anyone suggests something negative about the caregiver to them, they'll glom onto it as gospel, because they're looking for ways not to trust that person. They're looking for affirmation of their woundedness.

When this happens, telling the child that you understand his or her difficulties with trust issues is helpful; but it's counter-productive to argue about the issues at hand. It's not really about the issues—it's about trust.

Parental response

Patience is a good thing, but unless a parent comes from Mars, there's an end to it. Supporting an abuse victim through to recovery cannot mean allowing oneself to become abused in the process.

While it's necessary for a child to be able to exorcize his or her demons, it's not healthy for him or her to see the parent absorb the bile they are spewing. It has to be deflected. The child cannot be allowed to think that the fact that he or she was sexually abused is justification for verbally, physically or emotionally abusing someone else.

If you allow the survivor to make your life miserable, you will only add to his or her guilt and shame, knowing how unhappy he or she is making you.

There's a difference between standing by with loving strength, understanding the process while someone spews out the poison inside; and getting sucked in emotionally, taking the poison personally.

Standing by doesn't always mean staying in the same room. If patience wears thin, it's better to be honest and calmly say you love him or her but can't take anymore that day and simply walk away. The child needs to know that you have boundaries. You are not buying into it. The child is loved but the poison is being rejected. When that is clear, it's a step in eliminating the confusion.

Past—or present and future?

A predator can destroy the duration of time in a child's life when the abuse is happening—but beyond that, it is the choice of the child and his or her caregivers, how much more of their lives the predator can destroy.

A predator can go to jail, work through his issues, rebuild himself from the core, never have another incident of abuse in his life, never see the victim again and still see the destruction of the child's life.

How? Through the bitterness and hatred in the heart of the child.

A parent or caregiver who reinforces bitterness and hatred is terribly shortsighted.

There are times when a predator is so repentant that he turns his life around to the degree that the person he once was, exists only in the hearts of those who hate him. In other circumstances, another predator may nurture the vile aspects of his soul and become increasingly evil.

The way a victim lives life beyond the period of abuse really has nothing to do with the perpetrator nor the way his life develops. In many cases, the perpetrator is never seen again by the victim. The only connection between the two dwells in the mind of the survivor. It's about the choice of a survivor to reach out for a new tomorrow—or to remain trapped by yesterday in shackles of unforgiveness, resentment and bitterness.

Forgiveness

If forgiving meant condoning, no one should ever forgive child sexual abuse. It is probably the worst crime imaginable, to selfishly satisfy one's own lusts through the use of an innocent child. It can't be condoned.

If forgiving meant forgetting, how could anyone ever forgive the very thing that has most negatively impacted his or her life? It's impossible to forget something like that.

If forgiving meant overlooking, it wouldn't happen. No one in their right minds could overlook something as heinous as child molestation and the suffering it entails.

If forgiving meant re-entering a relationship with an abuser just as though nothing had happened, it would be ridiculous. It did happen and it was enormously destructive.

Forgiveness is not about condoning, forgetting or overlooking what the perpetrator did, or necessarily hanging out with him again. It's about setting oneself free from the bitterness that can enslave one to past circumstances and people. Misunderstanding the meaning of forgiveness can keep victims unnecessarily trapped in unforgiveness and hatred all their lives.

Forgiveness is not a benefit to the abuser—it is a benefit to the survivor, in terms of letting go of the bitterness and pain the abuser caused. In order to go on with life in freedom and productivity, the survivor must let go and leave it all for God to figure out.

God says that vengeance is His and He will repay the evil that has been done in the world. We don't have to live our days haunted by the past.

We have a justice system that takes care of predators. Unforgiveness can't do the job of the courts. No one who has never experienced prison can imagine just how cruel and degrading that punishment can be. Sex offenders will pay for their acts for the rest of their lives, through all they have caused and lost as convicted criminals and through the shame and worry of being on the sex offender list.

Without forgiveness, we fill our minds with darkness and block any hopes for the future with hatred, thus giving ourselves to offenders to destroy us emotionally and spiritually as well as physically. We give them more power than they ever thought of.

Forgiving does not mean that we have to put ourselves in old positions of peril that could endanger us again. It doesn't even mean that we have to have any kind of relationship with the perpetrator again. That is a choice. If circumstances change to the degree that a survivor would feel safe with the person who abused him or her, there could be reconciliation—but only as a result of the expressed wishes of the survivor.

Some people feel that by not forgiving an offender, they have control or power over them. They think it gives them the right to demean, judge, gossip about or attack the offender. But it's all an illusion. No one can control another through unforgiveness. There are those who think they gain moral superiority by demeaning other – but if that's their only ticket to moral superiority, it won't take them far and they won't find that priceless inner peace.

Forgiveness, on the other hand, does give people power—power to rise above anything that anyone may throw our way, power to live in peace, power to escape the constraints of toxic thoughts.

Despite all the benefits of forgiveness, counseling a survivor to forgive too quickly can be a tremendous affront to him or her. Even if people understand the real purpose and meaning of forgiveness, it can be overwhelming to consider. Forgiveness is not something that can be pushed, forced or flogged. It has to happen individually as a personal choice when the right time comes – and it has to be understood.

I found it humanly impossible to forgive my son's abuser. When I found out what happened to my son, I was so devastated that I curled up in a fetal position inside and unconsciously built thick walls around my heart to protect me from life. While I functioned robotically, somehow managing to look after my home and family, I felt separated from the human race. I was locked up inside and didn't think I could ever smile again.

For a whole year, I lived like that. I knew I had to forgive and I tried to do it, but life was so painful that I had to keep those thick walls intact. Had anyone asked me, I would have said that I had forgiven the man, because I had spoken the words several times and I couldn't achieve any greater degree of forgiveness than I had already tried to give.

It was only through inviting two other women to pray with me that those walls began to come down. As they prayed, I was terrified as I felt the huge blocks beginning to crumble in a way I couldn't control. I could actually see myself as a little naked child curled up behind those thick walls, but as the women continued to pray, I was totally unable to prevent a brilliant light from slowly disintegrating the blocks. It was very, very frightening and I wanted, more than anything in the world, to keep those walls up.

Finally, the walls lay in piles of rubble all around me and clouds of dust obscured my ability to see. As they cleared, I actually saw Jesus approach me and I stood up, now dressed in a little white gown. He reached out and took my hand and we walked out of that prison hand in hand, over the rubble of the walls.

As that happened, a tremendous peace enveloped me. Every cell of my being relaxed. I was free. I had let go. I had finally forgiven. I shall never forget that day. The grass was greener; the sky was bluer and there was a song in my heart.

I believe that it was because of that unique experience of

forgiveness over twenty years ago, that I have been able to live in a state of forgiveness with other situations in my life.

Kia, one of the contributors to the insights in this book, told me about her ability to forgive her husband after he was convicted of child molestation.

> I experienced forgiveness as soon as the words of my husband's confession entered my conscious mind. Whether in or out of jail, he will be paying for his crime for the rest of his life. No matter how forgiven he may ever be by anyone, he cannot undo what he has done. Life will never return to 'normal' for him or for any of us. I don't have to hold onto him through bitterness to make him pay. My bitterness would punish only me. Other people may be able to forgive on their own, but for me, it took God's help. Genuine forgiveness, for me, was a supernatural work of grace.

The thing about forgiveness is that you don't have to feel it right away. You just have to want to forgive and decide to do it. The feelings will follow in the proper time.

Our emotions need to be the cabooses in our lives and the decisions we make, the engines. Too many people live the other way around, with their emotions as the engines, dragging them through life.

The confusion of misplaced guilt

I believe that many victims of abuse share a memory of the haunting moment when they could have prevented the abuse. If only they had screamed, run away, told someone, hit the offender—anything—anything to have retained their sense of self. That's why they often feel the confusing guilt of complicity in the abuse. They may feel that they allowed themselves to be trapped by the hunter and fell headlong into his snare, only to find themselves used by a manipulative, selfish predator.

Misunderstanding about the dynamics of abuse can take time, sometimes years, to sort through – particularly when the abuser is a beloved member of the family.

Rushing the healing process is not productive. No one but the victim can tell when it's time to take the next step to deeper understanding and truth.

People cannot articulate what they don't understand. Pushing may invite denial or psychological issues. That's why I caution against trying to rush healing. When it happens naturally, the healing is complete. Otherwise, the abuse may appear to be healed, but the infection will just come out another way.

Listen and love unconditionally

What struck me about the story of the Smart family was the depth of understanding and the dignity accorded to Elizabeth's little sister. No matter how desperate the family was for details, they restrained themselves and waited for the identification to emerge when Mary Elizabeth's mind had had time to process the input.

Their restraint paid off. The day came when she was able to remember and the rest is history. The face of the kidnapper went out over the news programs and it wasn't long before the miraculous reunion took place.

When the family was reunited with Elizabeth, they simply surrounded her with love and the story gradually unfolded.

Many victims of abuse hide their stories for years, fearing that if they tell anyone, they will be shunned, shamed, rejected and cut off from normalcy.

A loving environment where a victim feels safe to say anything he or she needs to say is like gold. Perhaps the greatest need of survivors is to feel that they are precious, no matter what has happened. When they see that others will allow them to express the feelings they see as so unacceptable—the fear, the rage, the betrayal, the isolation, the depression, the guilt, the hatred, the shame, the worthlessness and the confusion—feelings of worth, love, acceptability, healing and forgiveness can begin to resonate within them.

Don't be surprised if the kinds of hugs and affection that come naturally to healthy people, don't seem to happen so often with a victim of abuse. It's not that they don't love you; it's just that the sense of touch has been perverted in their lives. It's natural for them to hug woodenly if they hug at all. It takes a long time to reestablish trust.

Forget the hammer

Men want to fix things. That's just how they're built. They respond to relationship problems the same way they respond to loose floorboards. Give them a hammer and some nails and they'll fix 'em. It's their comfort zone. Process is a foreign concept to them. They struggle with it.

Women, on the other hand, are more inclined to understand the process involved in getting things done. That's why they're often thought of as the more understanding gender—because to them, all of life is a matter of process.

One of the worst things one can do, when trying to help a loved one heal, is to "try to fix things." Offering solutions to someone who just wants someone to listen and validate their feelings, can result in the survivor simply shutting down. A solution may be as clear as glass to you and as logical as the path from A to B—but advice, particularly from loved ones, can come off sounding like criticism. It's all about unrushed process, the validation of the survivor's feelings and the sense of feeling precious to the listener.

It has taken me a long time to understand that when we give unsolicited advice, we send the message that the other person is incapable of making his or her own decisions. We reinforce their feelings of worthlessness. No matter how much we may love our families, we will reap only resentment if we imply that we know what is best for their lives. We have to be patient and love them enough to give them time to find the answers deep inside.

Therapy?

By not pushing or not rushing, I don't mean that a survivor should just be left to his or her own devices to heal. Not at all. If – *if* – a good therapist can be engaged, it can be helpful because they are not emotionally involved and can therefore suggest direction more freely than can someone in a subjective role.

Finding a good therapist, however, can be a real challenge. There's no point in wasting time. If the survivor does not seem to be making headway with a particular therapist, it may help to look for one who is more in tune with you or the victim. Just because someone has been recommended or has a good reputation, does not mean that person is right for you or your loved one.

Amazing developments

Through amazing developments, productive therapy is no longer just a protracted process of digging up and working through painful memories. Years of clinical experience and extensive research have resulted in proven methods for bringing great relief and healing to abuse victims. How people experience memories and triggers that act as reminders of the abuse can now be transformed. The two treatment approaches that appear to be most studied and supported by research are:

- Eye Movement Desensitization and Reprocessing (EMDR)
- Prolonged Exposure (PE)

Both of these treatments expose the patient to distressing aspects of memory in a safe, structured setting. Thousands of therapists around the world practice EMDR and can be found on the Internet through the EMDR International Association. My point in mentioning these treatments is not to go into detail about how they work—only to say that there are relatively rapid ways to deal with intensely distressing memories without having to be tortured by them for the rest of one's life.

Exploiting child sexual abuse

Like the lawyer who runs to the car accident, shoving his card in the pocket of a bloody victim, unscrupulous professionals can be found in abundance, networking through the halls of justice. Opportunistic psychotherapists and aggressive attorneys have built an industry out of child sexual abuse. They need victims to expand their domain. It has become common to hear of adults in psychotherapy suddenly recalling abuse that they later determine never happened. The "false memory syndrome" has become a common experience, generated by psychotherapists who "manufacture" victims.

Hopefully, professionals who would stoop so low are in the minority of the industry, but it's important for people in vulnerable situations to recognize the possibility of their presence.

Rather than routinely thrusting a newly discovered victim into therapy, each case should be approached in an individually sensitive way. There are children for whom reliving the event can be harmful, as therapy can heighten the event in the child's mind and interfere with the natural healing process.[82] The overreaction of parents, police and therapeutic intervention can worsen the situation. In his book, *What You Can Change and What You Can't*, M. Seligman recommends that parents, "Turn the volume down as soon as possible,"[83] lest they aggravate a negative reaction to the abuse.

Child sexual abuse is not a psychiatric problem or a disease. It is an event in a person's life. If there is demonstrable harm, like depression, sessions with a reputable therapist are no doubt in order.

Unfortunately, those of us who are sympathetic to the plight of victims and do not begrudge one cent spent on a genuine healing process, foot the bill for this increasingly out-of-control industry.

Also unfortunate is the tarnish the opportunistic professionals are

---

82. Bushman, B.J., Baumeister, R.F., & Stack, A.D. (1999). Catharsis, aggression and persuasive influence: Self-fulfilling or self-defeating prophecies? Journal of Personality and Social Psychology, 76, 367-376.
83. Seligman, M.E.P. (1994). What You Can Change and What You Can't. New York: Alfred A. Knopf.

putting on the wonderful work accomplished by the genuine heroes in the field.

Intervention

If your survivor is an adult who has not yet worked through the issues, an intervention may be required. He or she may be so miserable that being faced with a group of people who gather to express their love and concern may be the flash point that persuades him or her to seek treatment.

There are times when even an intervention evokes no response. It may seem that the loved one just flails away at life, refusing to respond to anyone. In certain cases, people need to fall flat on their faces, sometimes over and over again before they sincerely reach out for help. In such situations, all one can do is pray and be there when the time comes.

Prayer

While it has been obvious throughout this book how important a role faith plays in my life, I did not set out to write a "religious" book, because the scope of this topic reaches far beyond questions of faith. Nevertheless, I would short-change readers if I did not mention the importance of prayer in the healing process.

I have no idea how prayer works. All I know is that it was God's idea and it changes things.

All through history, people have believed that they can speak directly to God through prayer. If there had not been consistent response, surely people would have stopped such a strange, unnatural exercise eons ago. As a pragmatist, I certainly would have stopped. We are not a stupid species—well, not always. There has been consistent response to prayer, as evidenced by miracles and life-changing events throughout the history of the earth.

In the process of healing from abuse, prayer is particularly helpful because of trust and abandonment issues. The horror and shame prevents many victims from speaking to other humans. Knowing that God is ready to listen 24/7 can be enormously comforting. If we can't trust Him, whom can we trust? He alone has the power to change circumstances and intervene in situations that would seem impossible in human understanding.

For those who don't know how to pray, it may help to know that some of my most quickly answered prayers have been starkly simple, sometimes as short as, "Help!" Learning to pray is not a matter of memorizing liturgy. It's just a matter of practicing the presence of God in your life to the extent that you know He's at your elbow every moment and is just waiting to hear you speak to Him the way you would speak to anyone you respect and love.

It is a shame that people have strangled the flow of prayer through man-made traditions and rules. The examples God gave us were simple communications from our hearts to His.

Sometimes, answers to prayer appear suddenly, as miracles. In other situations, they come over a period of time as we continue to pray about the situation, day after day after day.

I have no idea how I would have survived all of the drama of my life without the availability of prayer.

The story of Sandra[84]

When Sandra was a young girl, she was molested and used by her father from about the age of ten until she found a way to protect herself when she was about 17-years-old. Here is her story.

D. Can you tell me a little bit about your family background?

S My brother and I were raised in an environment of fear. My father was a very dominating, intimidating man. Children were to be seen and not heard. I knew we were loved, but there was a lot of harshness. My father's mother had been quite brutal with him. He had a lot of violence in his background and then he had abandonment issues with her dying early. But as a child, none of that meant anything to me. All I knew was that I was frightened.

My mother was a very passive woman. But passive-aggressive. Like a lot of women back then, she found her own ways of coping. We had a large extended family on my mother's side, not so large on my father's side. They were all regular working-class people. There were really no church-goers among us.

D. Were any of the extended family aware of the abuse you were suffering?

S. I used to wonder about that. There was a couple, lovely people in the community who befriended my family, who had an uncanny ability to show up and whisk me away for an outing just when I thought I coudn't take the environment any longer. It was just all about my fear, living in fear. They would just show up. I could hear that woman's heels coming on the sidewalk.

84. Name changed to protect identity.

One of my best memories was the sound of her heels coming. And she would say, "How about we take her off your hands for a little while?" And they would take me to their house. It was a spotless little home. Oh...that was the safest place in all the world. When I grew up, I fished around a little bit to find out if they knew, but they didn't.They knew he was mean and harsh to us and that my mom had a hard life with him. Her coming and taking me away was what they could do.

I have since spoken with a few of my aunts who admitted that they wondered about it and perhaps all knew deep down. When I asked why nobody ever came to help me, they said it was because they were all afraid of my dad. He was such an intimidating man. In the fifties, people didn't interfere in each other's lives. There were boundaries and you just didn't go there.

D. When did the sexual abuse begin?

S. I was just entering the seventh grade and my mother sent me in to my dad. Prior to that, she used to tell me to go in and have a nap with my dad, and so I'd lie down beside him and we'd have a nap. That is totally inappropriate behavior for a young girl to be lying down on the same bed as her father. Or if he was watching TV, he'd get me to sit beside him and cuddle. The thing that I was always afraid was going to happen, my mom actually initiated.

D. Your feelings toward her must have been as difficult towards her, or even more difficult than they were towards your dad.

S. They were probably more difficult when I got old enough and started to understand. I remember being so frightened the first night she sent me in. I still remember exactly what time it was...

the clock on the wall. My dad was a shiftworker and if he was wakened early, there was always a price to pay. My mom was making his lunch and it was about 30 minutes before he was to be wakened that she sent me in.

D. And you think she knew what she was doing?

S. Oh, yes, she knew. Once when I tried to talk to her about it, she slapped me across my face and she would never normally do that. That was when I knew that the door was closed to talking to her.

No one discussed things like that in those days. I was in my twenties before I even knew there was a name for what happened to me. I was listening to the radio and thought the topic they were about to discuss was insects. I didn't want to listen to a show about bugs, but suddenly realized that they were talking about my life and the word was "incest." I was shocked to know that other people shared my experience.

Those were very different days. In a strange way, I believe that my mother did the best she could in the circumstances she was in and with the resources available to her. My father was the one with all the power and so she had to be a victim. It was all about survival for her.

D. When your father was molesting you, how did it make you feel as a person? How did you survive it? Where did you go in your mind?

S. If you talk to prostitutes, they will tell you that they disappear. They go somewhere else in their minds. You find a way to cope. Many people who have been abused say that just because your body may respond during abuse, doesn't mean that you like it. But the fact is that if you're being masturbated, then you're going to think that you must like it. But I hated my body so much. I would stand in my closet and bang my head against the closet wall. Then, when I was an adult, I had headaches a lot and tests showed that I had all these hairline fractures from all those years of banging my head against the wall—because there has to be some way to feel as bad on the outside as you do on the inside. I hated my body and I hated that I was a woman. I became anorexic. That is a way for people who feel they don't have control to get control in some area. I went down to 83 pounds at my lowest, but hung around 86 pounds in the years I was anorexic. Of course I was emaciated, so I had no breasts. My father stopped molesting me when I was really emaciated. I was probably 17. That was when a very powerful tool kicked in. I discovered that if I could be emaciated and look androgenous, no one would hit on me. I cut my hair. I wore men's shirts. I wore straight-leg jeans. That was an amazing tool for hiding myself away. I have spoken to many women who have done the same thing with excess weight.

Those were horrible, horrible dark years. I used to think about what it would be like to kill him because he was a hunter and the guns were kept in my closet. But then I'd think that I'd have to shoot my mother because she couldn't live without him, and then I'd have to shoot my brother because he couldn't live without her. When I was young, those were my thoughts, but I understand now why people shoot their whole family, not just one person—and it's sad that I understand. I fantasized about it. I was suicidal. I was so broken. How I got through those days... I had horrific reoccurring nightmares.

They were dark, lonely frightening days, so dark that I didn't know how I would go on. They were so dark that I alternated between rage when he wasn't around and fantasies about killing him.

D. Did you ever try to resist him?

S. Yes, not in any physical way, but I used to pretend that I was asleep a lot—but that wouldn't work because he knew I wasn't really sleeping. When I pretended to be asleep too many days in a row, then the tension in our home got so great that he would pick on my brother and my mother, so I knew what I had to do. My whole belief system was that I was keeping my brother and my mother safe. That was the lie, and so that kept me doing what I was doing. I thought if I did it, my mother would be okay, but it was a lie, because none of us were okay. That's why I kept letting it happen.

And then the more complicated issue is acceptance. Parental love and acceptance is critical and you'll take it at whatever level it comes to you. My self-concept was unbelievably low. I had no boyfriends and my father suggested that we could put an ad in the paper for one. When your own father tells you that the only way you're going to get a boyfriend is by putting an ad in the paper and he's molesting you and your mother is letting him... it's amazing that I can walk and chew gum!

And then began the huge journey. When I finally got the courage to leave, I started to make some really stupid decisions.

D. How long did you live at home after you became emaciated and your father stopped abusing you?

S. Probably about six or seven months. I found a job in another city. I felt wretched about leaving my mother and brother alone.

It was a very, very hard decision to make. My brother was two years younger and he left not too long after that.

I started to date a really decent guy, but left him for a married man I was working with. He was abusive, but it was more my fit. So I understand how abused people make extraordinarily stupid decisions. If somebody was abusing me or cheating on me, then I could live with that, because that's what I thought I deserved. It was my comfort zone.

D. You never involved the justice system?

S. No. I never even knew until several years later that there was a name for what had happened to me. I did go back to talk to him about things, but it turned into a confrontation and didn't go well so my father asked me to leave.

D. What has turned things around for you? You are so strong and beautiful and feminine and you have such a wonderful family. How did the change come?

S. I made some friends at work. The wife of one of them became a Christian and wanted me to go to church with her. She was amazing. She bought Christian albums for me that kind of mirrored the music I was listening to, but with a Christian message. Some years before, my grandfather had had a "born-again" experience and talked to me about it, but I didn't really understand what that meant. I think I had been searching, but this woman was wonderful. After I broke up with the married man I had been living with, I lost my apartment to him and had nowhere to go, so she took me in. I started to go to cell groups at her church and became a Christian. I met Sam (my husband) there. The vey first night he took me home, I unloaded on him in the car and told him everything. I had never told anyone before.

We have learned so much about inner healing together because of what we've gone through in the process of my healing. I think I will always have a level of grief that Sam had to go through my healing process with me.

D. How did your abuse affect your marriage relationship?

S. Oh, on every level. Physical intimacy was very, very hard. There were trust issues. That kind of pain and rage has to go somewhere if it has permission to go somewhere, and once I found out that Sam was a safe place to put it, he got a load of stuff that didn't belong to him—so every poor behavior that I had ever wanted to try on, I tried on with him.

Because of my level of brokenness, I was very fragmented and had developed some pretty complex personalities in order to survive. And then there was the issue of adultery. If you have incest in your life, you have to deal with adultery issues. I was my father's other woman, whether I meant to commit adultery or not. When I came out of the bedroom, my mother hated me. She would never speak to me for the first fifteen minutes. It was a very complicated situation. I used that power against her because I knew I could get him to do things for all of us that she couldn't get him to do and that's a terrible power to give to a child. I know I used that against my mother—not on purpose—but I know I used that against her. That's a terrible thing to do to another woman, a terrible thing to do to your mother. But that's the reality of it and I know that it functions where there's incest, whether with a step-parent or with a biological parent. It leads to very unusual choices that you make later in life.

D. Do you feel that you would have gotten through to this place of healing without prayer?

S. No, I don't. There was demonic interference in my life.

D. What about the secular treatments? Can they not work?

S. Certainly they can work. I think there's a wideness to the graciousness of God. There are all kinds of ways for healing to happen, but I think that if you have a demonic stronghold in your life, you will battle that. I did get into Christian counseling and I was on anti-depressants. I've done it all, because it takes awhile to get that broken and it takes awhile to get that fixed.

D. Do you feel healed?

S. Yes, I really do. I have walked through so much. My father came to me three years after I got married. I had never been alone with him. I didn't go and put myself at risk after I found that I could be safe. I had Sam to protect me. I had a husband, someone looking out for me—but I had gone to visit them and was choosing to stay overnight with them for the first time. My father asked me to go outside with him and I was terrified. I didn't know what he wanted to do. We went out to the backyard and he said, "I have something to say to you." He asked me to forgive him. It was really, really profound. He was so broken. He said, "I did the worst thing a father could ever do to a daughter."

I said, "Dad, I forgave you. I told you that years ago." He said, "Well, I want to ask you to forgive me." I said, "Dad, I forgive you. What your next step needs to be is to ask God to forgive you." He said, "God could never forgive a man for doing what I've done to you." I said, "Actually God could, and someday I hope you'll know what that would be like."

It was all he could do to ask that of me. Sam and I did a lot of prayer because I knew there was a lot keeping my dad from getting himself right with God. We saw that every time we visited, things were a little bit better. Once when we were there, I was cross country skiing with my kids and I felt like I should talk to him alone, so I asked my mother to watch the kids and asked my dad to go for a ski with me. It was one of those March days when it was so glorious that you could sing. We had done a few runs up and down the hills when I was on the top of a hill and I wasn't afraid of him for the first time in my life. I was 34 years old and I wasn't afraid. I looked at him and I said, "I'm not afraid of you. For the first time in my life, I don't think you'll ever hurt me again.

He started to cry. He put his arms out and I stepped into his arms and he held me and for the first time in my life I knew what it was like to be held by a father who wouldn't hurt you. I'll never forget that—the canvas of his coat. He wore these leather gloves that I wear now, the lumberman's gloves with the mit and the one thumb and they're all deer leather.

We didn't say anymore. He was undone and I was undone—I didn't know what to think, so I went and got the kids in the car and went home.

That was the first time that I could ever think of calling God, "Father." It was so profound. My prayer life changed.

D. You spoke of the difference between identifying yourself as a victim or a survivor and being an overcomer. Could you expand on that?

S. There's a process of moving from victim to survivor to overcomer. When people start to identify themselves as survivors of sexual abuse, they're not always the nicest people. They think they've survived abuse, it no longer has the power to sink them. They've survived it and lived through it, but it's still their identity. Their identity is in their past. They don't have an identity that's separate from their past because their responses are tied to what happened to them in the past. So even though they might have walked away from it and determined no one will ever do anything to them again, they are responding and reacting to life out of what has happened to them.

People who call themselves survivors are so busy identifying themselves by what has happened to them, it's all about their past, whether they're trying to redeem it or not. They are often very self-absorbed. If you're identifying yourself as a survivor, you're actively working to keep yourself safe so that you're probably always anticipating the next bad thing. It means taking a defensive posture through life.

Becoming an overcomer means moving away from the survivor mode, away from feeling identified by one's abuse, into a different place. My identity now is not in my past, but in who God has made me through all this. And that's how the step is taken from survivor to overcomer—it's by understanding that what your past was doesn't have to identify everything about who you are now. To overcome, you have to get over something to find a higher perspective and I think it's extraordinary grace that lifts us up to the place where we can say, okay, now I can see it from here. It's above the place where you always expect things to happen or being on guard. Overcoming is a goal.

I actually used to tell people when I would meet them, that I am a victim of incest. They didn't want to know that, but I'd tell them anyway. Then there were years when I'd tell them I was an abuse survivor. Now extraordinary grace has brought me through to the place of overcoming and I don't need to tell anyone about what happened to me—unless I feel it will help them in their own journey of healing..

D. On behalf of all who will read your story and find the words healing, thank you Sandra.

David's Sword[85]

David Elliot, (at this writing) 11-years-old, was molested by an older boy when he was eight. Four months after the abuse began, David summoned the courage to go into his parents' bedroom one night and tell them what was happening to him.

Rather than shove the horror under the carpet, these wise parents gently guided David to a place of using what had been done to him to help other children who have suffered similar devastation in their young lives. Together, they wrote a wonderful little book, *David's Sword*, which has received high praise from counselors and educators in their work with children. The Elliots recently gave an update on David's progress:

> David was in counseling for 20 months. He still has some off-days. He struggles with some terms and phrases that pull back memories from the past. But he also now will say "this may be a remnant." He is learning the skills to recognize and implement the strategies he has been taught, to deal with these feelings and issues as they arise. He continues to talk as the occasion arises, and found out from an email that he was instrumental in saving an 11-year-old boy's life who had experienced this, and was contemplating suicide. Through David's book, he has garnered strength and is talking, journaling and seeing his counselor to work through this and learn the skills to help him have the life

9. Tate Publishing & Enterprises, LLC, 127 E. Trade Center Terrace | Mustang, Oklahoma 73064 USA, 1.888.361.9473 | www.tatepublishing.com

he deserves. David said "Mom if this book helps only this boy, it was all worth it."

One would think that child sexual abuse is one of the worst things that can happen to a child. However, one would think that the smashing of a glass would be the worst thing that could ever happen to a glass—until the pieces are placed in the hands of the great Artisan and we wait patiently while he places the pieces, one by one, into the wonderful mosaic He envisions.

I am not saying that God plans for some people to be abused. I am saying that when we place the circumstances of our lives in His hands and give up natural inclinations like hatred, unforgiveness and bitterness – health and beauty can emerge.

By reinforcing hatred and unforgiveness, our children will remain broken. Through unconditional love, wisdom, guidance and forgiveness, the beautiful mosaic of their lives will gradually become visible. The past is irreparable—but the future is available.

8 eight

Smart Justice

Round 'em all up, throw 'em behind bars and leave them to rot, never to see daylight again.

That's not far from the sentiments most of us have with regard to child molesters. The very thought of touching a child sexually is so abhorrent to a healthy person that we instinctively want to banish anyone who might behave in a contrary manner to our natural responses of protection towards children. And the fact is, for violent, repeat offenders, it's a no-brainer. It stands to reason that unrepentant, sadistic child molesters need to be locked away from society where they can never again harm a child.

But not all child molesters are serial sadists. Every week, we see senators, teachers, doctors and even judges, led in handcuffs from their homes to waiting squad cars. It goes without saying that their status in life should not have any bearing on their punishment. But despite the fact that the fallout from their offences can be absolutely devastating, they will eventually be released from prison.

According to most people, treatment for pedophilia and child molestation begins with arrest and ends with imprisonment.

They don't think beyond the prison sentence to the time when the offender will be set free. But we have to be clear-headed and prepared to receive these people in the most constructive way—the way that will bring the greatest promise that they will not re-offend when the justice system is finished with them. These individuals need to be approached as individuals who will respond in individual ways to individual types of treatments. While they may bear the same scarlet letter, there are important differences that impact the possibility of functioning safely in society – thereby impacting the possibility of safety for children.

We try people within the court system; a judge determines the length of time criminals need to stay behind bars to pay for their crimes—and then we let them out. We say, "Go and make a living, don't be a drain on society and don't ever bother us again—and, oh yeah—stay away from our kids!"

But even for those who have learned their lessons in prison and are determined never to offend again, reconstructing their lives is not a straightforward process—a fact which can lead to re-offending. By the time the majority of child molesters leave prison, they have lost their structures. Everything is gone—families, homes, careers, vehicles, names, credit ratings, savings and friends. They are outcasts from society. People don't want them living in their neighborhoods. Those who willingly interact with them are often paid professionals whose job it is to assist with their reintegration into society.

And so, after varying degrees of failed efforts to reestablish themselves, some child molesters become so disheartened that they give in to the old temptations and re-offend, as is shown by some studies which claim a high degree of recidivism (repeat offending) resulting from the present approach to justice.

The high cost of recidivism

When a child molester re-offends, the greatest cost is to the children who are victimized. A victimized child, by no fault of his or her own, is set on a life course that should never have faced him or her. The path of healing is long and arduous and, for some, never ends. Everything is affected—relationships, ability to concentrate, ability to trust, self-esteem—and it goes on, as shown in the list of effects detailed in Chapter One: "Why All the Fuss?" – Prevalence, Effects and Trends of Child Sexual Abuse.

Then there's the cost to the families of both the victims and the offenders. While they may not be the primary victims, they are clearly secondary victims. Life becomes about helping the children to heal and coping with one's own grief—or coping with the horror, grief and fallout of having a loved one revealed to be a predator.

Then there's the cost to all of society—not only the direct costs of maintaining inmates and penal systems, but all the secondary costs as also outlined in Chapter One.

Preventing recidivism (repeat offending)

Thus, it seems to me that prevention of recidivism should be an *enormous* priority in society.

It goes without saying that the first line of offense has to be prevention of the first incident of sexual child abuse in terms of both protecting children and preventing our sons, daughters, husbands, wives, brothers, sisters and neighbors from becoming abusers.

But if the unthinkable has already happened, if someone has molested a child, we must make sure it doesn't happen again. How do we do that?

We have to push past our natural inclinations and be smart about how we treat offenders when they get out of prison. Knee jerk reactions just drive the problems deeper.

When first line prevention hasn't worked

At this point, jail sentences, parole and life on the sex offender registry are the judicial consequences for those who are caught. The length of the sentence and parole varies with the part of the world in which the person victimizes a child.

Depending on the degree of abuse administered and other factors, the sentence can be more or less severe. According to *Time* magazine, the average sentence in the U.S. is eleven years. In Canada, that can be considerably shorter as it is in many other countries.

For many, jail time can mean being subjected to repeated rapes and beatings by other prisoners who consider child molesters to be fair game, the lowest rung on the jailhouse status ladder—scapegoats for every injustice the other criminals have ever experienced in life. Because signing up for treatment can red flag their crime to other inmates who don't know what they've done, child molesters often choose not to seek treatment. The result can be that they finish their sentences either hardened, jaded and untreated—or broken – whether treated or untreated.

Then they get out.

Tim Danson is a Toronto lawyer who has been involved in representing the families of some of Canada's most notorious sex offenders. He wants a law that would allow authorities to detain high-risk offenders indefinitely or until such time as they could be shown not to be a threat. In an October 24, 2007 interview for the *Canadian National Post*, he claimed that such a law would give the system more latitude when dealing with less aggressive pedophiles. In a quote he said,

> "If the public knew that the real dangerous sexual predators were being locked up, there would be far greater tolerance for legitimate treatment programs for sex offenders who might be amenable to treatment."

Politicians and judges who dare to suggest there is a better way of dealing with child molesters than throwing them in the bull pens and seeing if they come out alive, risk being labeled as soft on pedophiles. Unfortunately, the public on whom politicians rely to keep them in office are not always well-informed on the issues.

The point is that people who have been convicted of molesting children are going to be released and it behooves us as a world community to do everything we can to make sure that they don't re-offend. That means indefinite incarceration for the worst and treatment for those who are salvageable.

Can treatment guarantee change?

There are few guarantees in life, but evidence gives grounds for hope and effort. Because the cognitive/behavioral analysis of how child molesters develop helps to explain why some adults are attracted to children, it also holds the critical promise that what has been learned can be unlearned.

The problem is that the stakes are so high and the issue is so fraught with tension that trial and error with what works and what doesn't work isn't an option.

We've all heard the rhetoric about the 95 percent recidivism rate and blanket statements about pedophilia being incurable. Most up-to-date studies reveal that to be reflex hype. For instance, a 2004 study done by the University of Toronto Department of Psychiatry concluded that the recidivism rate ranged from 84 percent to 94 percent after 25 years. Critics proved that that study of 340 sex offenders was *not* representative. Nevertheless, there is still disagreement among psychiatrists with regard to success rates with the various treatment options.

Some psychiatrists claim great success with the use of chemical castration, drugs and psychotherapy in converting the sexual preference of pedophiles from children to other adults. Others claim that it's not possible to entirely convert pedophilic preferences, but that good treatment will keep an individual from re-offending.

It seems that statistics in every level of this issue are practically worthless. Some experts say the rate of recidivism is 10 percent to 25 percent. As previously demonstrated, others claim that the rate is higher. Complicating the statistics are the categories of offence. For instance, it has been shown that incestuous predators are more successfully treated and less dangerous than true pedophiles who have victimized many children—some of them in the hundreds. But those statistics are useless when applied to child molesters who can be equally attracted to children and adults.

Dr. Paul Federoff, an Ottawa, Ontario psychiatrist, was interviewed by journalist Tom Blackwell in October of 2007. Dr. Federoff, through the administration of LHRH analogs, new versions of anti-androgen drugs (chemical castration drugs) developed to treat prostate cancer and cognitive therapy, claims that even true pedophiles can transform. His reasoning is that everyone was once attracted to children (when they were children themselves) but that these people have never developed out of that stage. He claims that it is a natural process to be changed.

It seems to be working. His patients who normally struggle in their battles with inappropriate urges, tell him that the drugs eradicate the urges to the extent that they feel as though they are "on vacation." The cognitive therapy and counseling towards a positive lifestyle with "age-appropriate" partners continue as the patients are gradually weaned off the drugs. Quoted in the *National Post*, Dr. Federoff said,

> "The idea that these sexual interests are unmodifiable, I think, is completely wrong. Not only can it be changed, it's a natural process to be changed."

In the same article, Mr. Blackwell interviewed Dr. Howard Barrbaree of Ontario's Centre for Addiction and Mental Health (CAMH). While Dr. Barrbaree does not claim any evidence to prove that pedophiles can be converted into people who prefer "age-appropriate" partners, he does say that

> "it is clearly possible to suppress the pedophile's sexual response to children through cognitive therapy."

Further, he claims that in 14 years of treating convicted pedophiles, CAMH has *no major* incidents of recidivism.

Dr. Karl Hanson of the Correctional Service of Canada, in a 2004 review of 10 studies in Canada, the United States and Europe, involving a total of 4,724 sex offenders, concluded that 13 percent of known child molesters re-offended after five years, 18 percent after 10 years and 23 percent after 15 years.

An integrated perspective - incarcerative punishment, psychiatric treatment and Restorative Justice

I believe that smart justice requires the integration of incarcerative punishment, psychiatric treatment and restorative justice.

Child molesters need to be locked up, not only to teach them a harsh lesson, but also to give a victim some sense of justice. Then, we need to take advantage of treatments that have been found successful and not leave it up to the offender to choose or not to choose treatment. It should be mandatory.

But we need to go further. We need to embrace the principles of restorative justice.

Why do we need more than prison and treatment?

As our justice system now stands, the entire focus is on the offender—what he or she has done, whether there will be a plea or a trial and, if found guilty, how long the sentence will be and where it will be served. Unless they testify or have reason to be in the courtroom, the victims remain faceless to the court system. Unless they arrange privately for therapy (which presents its own issues of isolation), they can be left entirely out of the loop with questions they deserve to have answered.

It seems to me that more needs to be done to heal the wounds of the people affected by the crime, to eliminate as much conflict as possible and to provide support and accountability for offenders so that the chances of re-offending will be lessened.

There are two sides to crime—the public and the personal dimensions. Our justice system is largely one dimensional, in terms of addressing public issues but not the personal issues.

When offenders are released, there needs to be an effective network in place for their successful reintegration into society. With the numbers of molesters coming up through the ranks, being groomed by the flood of pornography, we need to be preparing this network. Otherwise, society is going to be overrun by a huge number of ex-convicts who may re-offend, overburdening an already stressed public system.

What is "Restorative Justice?"

I first heard of restorative justice 'by accident.' I was talking to a colleague whose graphic design company 'just happened' to do some preparation of materials for the Community Justice Institute in Kitchener, Ontario. When I told her about my commitment to the prevention of child sexual abuse, she mentioned the CJI and suggested that I get in touch with them.

What followed was my introduction to a philosophy of justice that looks at the big picture and does what it can to bring healing to every level of involvement for the benefit of the entire society.

One little book of particular help to anyone seeking to understand the tenets of restorative justice was written by one of its founding developers, Howard Zehr. The book is called *The Little Book of Restorative Justice* and was published by Good Books, Intercourse, PA.

In the 1970s, recognition of the fact that the criminal justice system does not adequately deal with the fallout of crime, began to gel. Justice professionals and community workers began to look at models of justice that could work alongside the legal system to address the whole picture—to help restore victims and to help offenders become contributing members of society.

Restorative justice is really nothing new. Versions of it can be found here and there in history as cultural processes of conflict resolution and traditional justice. For instance, the First Nation communities in Canada used "circles" to work through conflicts in a community. In these "circles," participants gathered in a circle and passed a "talking piece" from person to person to ensure that only one person spoke at a time in the order in which they were seated. The community "elders" served as facilitators. The idea was to provide an opportunity for victims to express their depth of injury, for members of the community to gain understanding of their own roles in the situation and to determine how an offender could bring restitution to the victim and be restored to the community for its benefit.

In many places, restorative justice is being viewed as the wave of the future—the path to a more comprehensive approach to dealing with crime. In New Zealand, it has become the central approach to dealing with juveniles who offend. In Canada, public funding is gradually becoming available as the merits of the approach are becoming more and more recognized.

There are those who shy away from restorative justice, thinking it's just a front for going soft on offenders or pushing forgiveness down the throats of victims. It's neither of those. In fact, even the word "mediation" has been rejected by advocates of the approach, because the concept is more about opportunities to dialogue than to coerce wounded people into reconciliation.

Far from going soft on offenders, one of the main objectives is to get offenders to really understand what they have done to their victims, to the point that they experience real empathy. This is huge, I believe, because it seems to me that one of the most hurtful things a child molester does is to objectify his or her victims—to regard them as nothing more meaningful than a doll, a "thing" on which to carry out perverted fantasies. A victim can never feel that a perpetrator has any understanding of the depth of harm done, unless they see true empathy. That's impossible without (structured) contact.

An experience in jail is a great wake-up call for a child molester. No one will show him how reviled his behavior is as effectively as the other prisoners, to whom child molesters are the scum of the earth. However, as important as the wake-up call is, more is needed. Child molesters need to become accountable for their actions and prison does nothing to instill accountability. The shame instilled by the penal system needs to be transformed into a sense of responsibility to society to behave appropriately.

By encouraging offenders to develop personal abilities and skills, restorative justice assists with the transformation process which is critical for reintegration into society.

For anyone saying, "I don't want to help any child molester to end up with a good life," I say, "Give your head a shake! Wake up to the fact that the whole point is to do all we can to make sure it won't happen again!"

And then there's the family...

When a family member is discovered to be a child molester, it is as though an atom bomb has gone off in their midst. The sense of betrayal to the other members of the family is more than devastating on a multitude of levels. Concern for the victims is followed by deep grief over the loss of the family that is forever changed, forever deeply scarred by the horror of the actions of one of its members. Those who have worked hard to build solid lives feel that all of their efforts have been undermined – that their foundations have been suddenly eroded by a tsunami of shame.

Where a system of restorative justice in place following the release of the offender, the victims have an opportunity to ask questions that almost always still haunt them. The family has an opportunity to vent their pain in a constructive environment. There is a possibility of finding some closure to the trauma (in the sense of being able to better understand what happened and move forward). The offender has an arena within which to express the depth of his remorse to all involved. The victims have an opportunity to publicly express how deeply the offender's actions have affected their lives, thereby receiving some acknowledgement of their pain and return of control over their lives. While no apology could ever undo the crime, it can give the victims a sense of vindication and of having other people recognize the harm that was done to them. Restorative justice brings the perpetrator face to face with the damage done to the victims.

It would be wonderful if, one day, in every community, community justice institutes could be established to operate in cooperation with the present punitive system of justice, so that offenders would not only get the punishment they deserve, but the needs of everyone involved would be recognized and addressed for the benefit of all.

Recycling humanity

Recycling squished pop cans, discarded bottles, smeared news papers and broken cardboard has become de rigeur in our society.

But what about broken, smeared, squished and discarded humans? What do we do with them? There's no factory where they can be sent and magically turned into solid humans with no history or record of offending.

We have put great effort into making sure that we address all the issues in our planetary environment. We feel so environmentally evolved when we take our own natural fiber bags to the grocery store, drive our electric cars and recycle our disposables. We get a sense of contributing to a better world for our children!

Meanwhile, all across the country, child molesters who have served their time (many of whom have received no treatment in jail) are being released into our communities, emitting all nature of toxic fears into the hearts of mothers and fathers. People parade back and forth in front of the homes of ex-convicts, demanding their expulsion from the community, apparently not caring a fig if the kids where they end up are harmed. Are we that selfish? Do we care only about our own children and to heck with the kids in other communities?

The philosophy of restorative justice is great, but what about the logistics? Every released sex offender becomes somebody's neighbor. When forced to relocate, it is often to a poorer, more rural area with fewer resources to fight crime and provide treatment. When relocating an offender, would it not be more "environmentally friendly" to send a recycled, restored human to the new area rather than to irresponsibly shoo out a twisted, broken pedophile or child molester who could be deadly to a new location that lacks resources for treatment?

It doesn't make sense. We have to find a way of recycling the toxic waste of humanity into environmentally friendly people. And it can be done if approached with clear heads.

Supporting or shunning?

Perhaps one of the most ridiculous articles I have ever read appeared in an October, 2007 Toronto newspaper. It told of the development of a new community which is "officially free of sex offenders." Residents are routinely subjected to background checks and no one whose name appears on a sex-offender registry can purchase a home in the area. Beside the article is a woman standing in the new development with her arms crossed and a self-satisfied look on her face.

Little does that woman understand that the most dangerous people are the *undetected* pedophiles who live amongst us all—even in her structured community. People can live in the same house with a child molester for a lifetime with no idea of what is happening in their own homes! Don't get me wrong: I applaud those people for trying to protect their children, but the way they are going about it is at best selfish, and at worst, entirely ineffective.

Once a pedophile or a child molester is outed, they are at least known and can be dealt with. But then what do we do with them? What mother in her right mind is going to welcome a pedophile next door? The natural inclination is to shun, expel and rid the community of danger.

In several states in the U.S., real estate contracts contain a conditional clause that enables buyers to get out of a house deal if they discover that a sex offender is living too close to them for their individual comfort.

Plan to Protect™

It is totally impossible to identify a potential child molester or a pedophile who has not yet offended. If I can live with one for 38 years with absolutely no idea – until one of his victims had him charged and he finally admitted the truth – how can anyone be expected to recognize a predator? In the course of his confession, my (ex) husband explained that the reason I didn't see any evidence was that he was the world's greatest manipulator–a common characteristic of molesters.

If I could live so blinded with one *living right in my home* for 38 years, how would anyone in that structured community in Toronto – or anywhere – suppose they could recognize a molester next door?

I believe that a program such as *Plan to Protect™*, operated by *Winning Kids Inc.® (www.winningkidsinc.ca)* is the most effective tool to guard against potential molesters acting on their fantasies or molesters who have already molested but have not yet been caught, continuing their hidden criminal behaviour.

Plan to Protect is the protection plan being used in 3,500 churches, schools, associations and daycares to train everyone within the organization who either has access to children by means of their position within the organization, or who wishes to have access (through teaching, caretaking or some form of leadership) to such a position of trust. A high percentage of molesters see such positions as convenient blinds for their planned activities.

When it becomes obvious through the course of this mandatory training and screening that the price molesters (either potential or active) will have to pay if they get caught is too high to balance the "pleasure" of a few furtive moments, many potential molestations may be prevented.

That to me, is huge, because predators are so deceptive and manipulative that the only real way to change their behaviour is to change the hidden plans of their hearts.

Plan to Protect is a 250 page protection plan with policies, plans, training outlines, case studies, and 30 plus appendices to be used to establish a strong abuse prevention policy and program. The manual is widely used across the nation. While processing criminal record checks (in order to provide further evidence that the organization is doing everything within its ability to show that "Child Protection" is in place for insurance reasons) is part of the *Plan*, the reality is that a percentage of the trainees could be molesters with no criminal records that would show up.

Natural inclinations or wisdom?

We have to move beyond a culture of shame. History and research have shown that shaming someone drives them deeper into their addictions. As a society, to be effective in our response to offenders, our job has to be to lift people out of their addictions in structures of support. We have to suck it up—reject our natural inclinations to shun people who have behaved in ways that disgust us and find areas of integrity and health in their character on which we can focus and encourage them to build.

It's true that there are those who are so manipulative that they do not respond—but for those who truly want to rebuild themselves from the core, community support can mean the difference between success and failure.

Community support can be the key that prevents a molester from re-offending. Just one predator being turned around can save one or 10 or 100 children from being molested.

The best safeguards against child molestation lie within the hearts of reformed molesters – and within the hearts of potential molesters who are made to recognize the high cost they will have to pay for touching a child inappropriately.

When interviewed for an October, 2007 article in the *Canadian National Post*, clinical and forensic psychologist Dr. Robin Wilson (who has worked with more than 7,000 sexual offenders and is a consultant with a program called "Circles of Support") stated,

> "they are less likely to re-offend when provided with support outside of prison."

Circles of Support is an organization that began in 1994 in Hamilton, Ontario. Its philosophy is to surround released offenders with an inner circle of volunteers and an outer circle of professionals, rather than to shun them.

The inner circle is comprised of ordinary citizens who meet with offenders daily, helping them establish structures in their lives such as setting up banking, arranging transportation, getting car insurance and going to the laundromat. They seek to empower the participants rather than to make them dependant on the group.

When notorious child molester Charlie Taylor was released in the area, a local Mennonite Church accepted him into their congregation, treating him much the way they would their own families or friends. Until Charlie's death 11 years later, he lived without re-offending, a noteworthy accomplishment when the National Parole Board had given him a risk rating of 100 percent chance of re-offending within seven years.

Since its inception, the group has found that participants in the Circles of Support program have had a 70 percent reduction in re-offending. Two thirds of the participants said that on their own, they would have returned to crime.

According to Dr. Wilson,

> "This is a very simple concept. All we have to do is think of ourselves. We do well in life because we have people who care about us. If you're a long-term sex-offender and everyone in the community hates your guts and nobody wants to look at you, never mind spend any time with you, who's there to point you in the right direction when you make bad decisions?...The

> one thing about offenders that has probably struck me the most is just how exactly similar they are to the rest of us; that there is no tattoo in the middle of their forehead; there is no glaring difference between them and us that we can readily see. That dirty old man with the long greasy hair and dirty fingers in the park with bags of candy and a trench coat—he doesn't exist. Your average sex offender looks a lot like me; your average sex offender looks a lot like the Prime Minister; your average sex offender looks a lot like the next parent of a victim.... If we hide our heads in the sand and try and legislate them into non-existence, we're fooling ourselves. They're part of our community, and the only way we're going to get our heads around this is if we treat the problem as if it's a community issue."

The Circles of Support program is now partially funded by the Correctional Service of Canada.

According to the Jacob Wetterling Foundation, a Minnesota-based non-profit organization for the prevention of child abuse, formed following the abduction of young Jacob Wetterling,

> "Sex offenders are less likely to re-offend if they live and work in an environment free of harassment."[86]

RFID (radio frequency identification) bracelet or implanted chip tracking

There has been much discussion and sporadic testing of methods to keep track of predators following release. GPS offender

86. From the Jacob Wetterling Foundation web site's frequently asked questions section.

tracking technology, monitoring offenders day and night, raises the offender's level of responsibility for his or her own actions – which in turn protects the community.

The logic is that a sex offender is a suspect when any sexual crime is committed. Wearing an electronic bracelet would clear anyone who is under suspicion by providing proof positive of the person's whereabouts. Conversely, it would aid in apprehending the perpetrator.

When a crime occurs, the location of the offenders would be matched against a crime incident database to validate or rule out possible involvement by a particular offender.

Any released offender who truly commits to a changed life should be happy to wear one – for his or her own security as well as that of anyone else. A person can be continuously tracked without having their movements so restricted that they can't work or conduct a productive life. The implantation of a chip or the wearing of a tracking bracelet does not have to be visible to the public, thus allowing an offender to turn his or her life around, while ensuring optimal safety for children. GPS offender tracking technology monitors offenders day and night, raising the offender's level of responsibility for his or her own actions, which in turn protects the community. It's a way to keep our kids safe and allow a perpetrator who is truly trying to rebuild his life, "to live and work in an environment free of harassment."

If the rationale against permanent monitoring is based on the concept of freedom following the legally proscribed period of incarceration, I believe that the rationale is flawed. The nature of a crime against children requires special response in that the loss of trust is far more critical than with a thief who has stolen an object or a sum of money. Trust has to be built, earned and proven over time. It's not a gift.

Frankly, I believe that when a crime has been committed against a child, a perpetrator signs away his or her right to freedom for life - so freedom isn't my issue. My issue is with using wisdom in how we legislate the restrictions.

A public sex-offender registry

How does a public registry fit such a rationale? It eliminates freedom permanently and, according to my research, marginalizes released offenders to an extent that can endanger children.

In the spring of 2012, a website was launched by a Christian group in Alberta whose purpose is to make public the names and addresses of people who have been convicted of sex crimes against children. While this new site is not an *official* Canadian website, it will have the same effect – even though the information may not be as complete.

Until now, of all the countries in the world, only the U.S. has had a public registry where any citizen can do a search for predators in their area and find the details on each one. Nowhere else has the information on offenders been put on official websites.

Having tested the results of the public registry, there is now a huge movement in the U.S. to design better sex offender laws that lead to more constructive results (reformsexoffenderlaws.org).

In Canada, the national (non-public) sex offender registry came into force in December 2004, requiring convicted offenders to register within 15 days after being released from prison. Offenders are required to re-register annually, and re-register within two weeks of changing their home address. Only accredited police agencies have access to the information through the national sex offender database, maintained by the Mounties.

The launching of this new, private site gives rise to several questions. Will a public registry ensure the safety of children? What is the downside?

I believe public registries cause more problems than they solve, that children are actually placed at higher risk and such registries turn a certain element of society into packs of vigilantes.

Will a public registry really make for a better society? I don't think so. Judging from my research, it won't make our kids safer and it will encourage licence for a mindless pack-mentality. Justice needs to be smart. Justice needs to get the job of protection for our kids done right. Justice needs to foster effective vigilance - not vigilantism.

Jail-house religion—or restorative faith?

And what of "religion?" Can it make authentic changes in offenders?

It's a well-known fact that many inmates receive what is often referred to as, "jail-house religion," a focus on God as a lifeline of hope through the dark days behind bars.

For some, it's just a diversion, perhaps a manipulation to garner support or sympathy. There's no real depth to their avowed convictions. When they leave prison, they quickly forget what once appeared to be so important to them.

For others, there is a genuine gratitude for having been caught so that they can clean the slate and have another chance to make it right with God and whoever else will receive them. For these people, the roots can go deep and form the anchor for reestablishing solid lives upon release.

The reality, however, is that no matter how *God* may have forgiven these people, the people who line the pews aren't usually so quick to forgive and they generally shun the ex-convict from fellowship.

From the perspective of some offenders, hope for any sort of restoration dwindles. They eventually leave the church. The reality of God begins to fade without teaching and interaction of like-minded individuals, and again they may fall prey to old temptations.

Unfortunately, churches, like all of society, have high percentages of people who have never really known God and so cannot understand His ways. These churches have no ability to do the job they are meant to do in society. Their legacy to humanity is one of judgment, criticism, bitterness, disillusionment and isolation.

A few offenders are fortunate and find genuine fellowships of faith where there is honest recognition of equality before God. Where this happens, a system of accountability can be established and the ex-convict is given the opportunity to find dignity and restoration – critical factors in becoming people of integrity who can effectively contribute to society.

Such an establishment gives higher meaning to "a just society."

The responsibility of the church

By definition, it seems to me that the church does not have the option of holding its collective nose and turning away from the offender. Here is God's definition of functional religion:

> Religion that God our father accepts as pure and faultless is this: to look after orphans and widows in their distress and to keep oneself from being polluted by the world.[87]

> Remember those in prison as if you were their fellow prisoners, and those who are mistreated as if you yourself were suffering.[88]

The Apostle Paul, in addressing the importance of forgiveness, said,

> If anyone has caused grief, he has not so much grieved me as he has grieved all of you to some extent—not to put it too severely. The punishment inflicted on him by the majority (the courts) is sufficient for him. Now instead, you ought to forgive and comfort him, so that he will not be overwhelmed by excessive sorrow. I urge you therefore to reaffirm your love for him. The reason I wrote you was to see if you would stand the test and be obedient in everything. If you forgive anyone, I also forgive him. And what I have forgiven—if there was anything to forgive—I have forgiven in the sight of Christ for your sake, in order that Satan might not outwit us. For we are not unaware of his schemes.[89]

---

87. James 1:27, The New International Version, Zondervan Bible Publishers, Grand Rapids, Michigan.
88. Hebrews 13:3. The New International Version, Zondervan Bible Publishers, Grand Rapids, Michigan.
89. 2 Corinthians 2:5-11. The New International Version, Zondervan Bible Publishers, Grand Rapids, Michigan.

The XXX church

Pure Life Ministries,found on the web at www.purelifeministries.org, understands and deals with the sexual challenges of the twenty-first century in a right-on, realistic way. They shy away from nothing and are shocked by nothing. Their billboard sign reads, "The XXX Church!"

Pure Life Ministries do what they call "nouthetic counseling." To put it simply, nouthetic counseling consists of kindly confronting people with the teachings of Scripture out of genuine concern for the person, in order to help them make changes.

Their success rate is remarkable.

The Bursey model for re-integration into a church

About a month before one of the former members of his congregation got out of prison, Pastor Dean Bursey, a senior pastor in Ontario, began to prepare his church for integrating the man into their assembly.

While his initial proposal to the Board was met with some skepticism and concern, agreement was reached to formulate a contract for the fellow to sign which would establish boundaries to formalize expectations for his activities in the church.

One very interesting aspect of Dean's involvement was a vision he was given prior to the man's confession and subsequent need for reintegration into the community. I believe that this very unusual occurence prepared him for the challenges he would soon face with this fellow and those yet to come.The following is Pastor Dean's experience in his own words.

A Pastor's Perspective

I am not a mystical person who is prone to unusual experiences but I truly feel that God spoke to me one day in the same way that he spoke to Peter on the roof of Cornelius's house in Acts 10. The Acts experience was meant to take away Peter's prejudices against people of other cultures so he could minister more effectively to them. I believe that my experience was also meant to take away some of my prejudices and make me a more effective minister to all of God's people.

I was sitting in my office at the church one afternoon when our church secretary buzzed me from her office to inform me that a gentleman from our neighborhood had called requesting to meet with one of the pastors from our church. I was the pastor on call that day and after checking my availability she had told him to come right away. He was very distraught and with good cause. Over the last few weeks his name had appeared in the newspaper after it was alleged that he has molested several young children from the community. He was formally charged and released on bail. Having young children myself at the time I was very upset about the situation in the neighborhood and about the fact that this perpetrator was about to come into my office. I imagined that he was coming to purge his own soul and seek forgiveness that frankly, I was not in any mood to offer. I found myself getting more and more agitated as the time approached for his arrival. Deep on the inside anger began to well up to the place where I was afraid that if I came face to face with this man I would probably be very unkind in my words and actions. I sat down in my chair and began to think about my own children and the hurt that someone like this could cause in their lives and the havoc that his actions could wreak on other unsuspecting families. I was in no way ready to meet with this man and certainly not ready to minister the love of Christ to him.

As I sat in my chair I closed my eyes and whispered a prayer to God asking him for Divine resolve. I can honestly say that what happened to me in the next few moments has not happened to me before or since.

I closed my eyes and put my head back in my chair in an honest effort to relax myself and meditate on anything good that I could force through my mind. I don't think that I fell asleep but as I relaxed I began to see a picture in front of me that caused me great concern. Some may call it a vision, others a dream, but I call it one of God's teaching moments.

In my mind I saw a well-dressed man walking down the street in a quiet suburban neighborhood. He stood erect with his head thrown back and his chest proudly stuck out. As I looked closer I saw a dog leash in his hand and on the end of the dog leash was a very pitiful creature. It was not a dog or some other animal but another person. The person on the leash was beaten and bloody, with torn clothes and very matted hair. As the proud man walked down the street he would take a few steps pull hard on the chain then turn and kick the man on the leash for seemingly no reason. My anger began to grow towards the proud and violent man as my sympathy began to grow towards his victim.

As this scene unfolded something inside of me, that I believe to have been God's Spirit, posed two questions to me. The first seemed easy. *"Who are you mad at in this picture?"*

My response was quick and easy. "I am angry with the man who is inflicting the pain and keeping another man on a leash."

The second question changed the course of my life and ministry. *"Then why are you angry with the man on the end of the chain?"*

"I'm not," I strongly protested. The moment the words left my mouth I knew that I was wrong. Slowly I began to realize that this was exactly what I had been doing. The man on the leash was the man who was coming to see me. Through his own wrong choices and sin decisions he had placed himself in bondage to someone and something bigger than himself. We are all responsible for the hurt that we inflict on others no matter what our background and environment. I had been directing all of my anger towards this man.

The proud man is the enemy of our soul, Satan, who seeks to destroy every person created in the image of God. He is not a fictional character, as some would have us believe, but a strong force for evil in our world. If we are followers of Jesus we must admit that Jesus believed very strongly in his existence and his ability to destroy. People who abuse others are in his horrible bondage and in desperate need of freedom. I was totally overlooking this proud man in my distribution of anger. I know that ultimately we are all still responsible for the decisions that get us into bondage and the hurt we inflict on others. We cannot underestimate the power of this evil and controlling person.

My brief moment of Godly insight changed the way I embraced the man who came through my office door that day. I still saw him as a perpetrator who had damaged and even ruined the lives of innocent people. I still saw him as a person who should be punished for his actions. I also saw him as a man who had allowed himself to be seduced by someone much more powerful than himself. But I also saw him as human and frail and in bondage. But I also was able to see that evil thing that was behind all sin and every act of hurt. I began to feel sympathy and compassion towards this person and even to view him as redeemable. I believe that God, without absolving the abuser, had given me a new place to direct the anger that was still deep inside me and that still needed a place to vent.

I still get angry every time I hear of someone powerless being hurt by a more powerful abuser. I still get angry with those who abuse but it does not overwhelm me because I am able to direct some of that anger to a place where I believe it belongs. I am able to direct it towards the proud man and get on with the business of ministering to the broken: all the broken.

And then came another heartbreaking situation with another former member of my church who was suddenly revealed to be a predator. I had thought I had known him and his family well and *never* would have dreamt that he would one day confess to child molestation.

Towards the end of his period of incarceration, as I set out on the hour long drive to the penitentiary to visit him, I could not help but be thankful that this ritual would soon come to an end. He was being released and would soon start the long process of trying to make his way back into the main stream of society. I could not help but think how difficult that transition was going to be for him. Because of his admission and subsequent conviction he had lost his business, his home, his family and his marriage – not to mention his freedom, dignity and respect. I had watched him, over the months of incarceration, become unglued from everything in his life except his faith in God. Now he was in the last month of his sentence and I was looking forward to not making this long trek again.

As we sat on opposite sides of the glass and talked on the phone it was evident that he was facing the reintroduction back into outside life with a mixture of fear and excitement. He was understandably afraid of what he would face on the outside but he was also excited about the possibility of facing life without the deep hidden secret that he had carried for so long. Because of our long relationship of about 13 years, I was not surprised when he told me that he wanted to attend my church when he got out. While he and his former wife had remained members of my previous church, they had stayed in close touch with me and my family and often attended sevices in my new church. It was not until I was alone on the drive back to my office that I began to come to grips with the possible challenges connected to saying "yes" to his request and it was not until that moment that I knew in my heart that I had to include him in our church.

Leading a growing church is challenging at the best of times, but in the life of a church there are those unique situations that stretch a pastor and leadership beyond the natural. The re-introduction back into the life of a church, of a person who has been convicted of child molestation, is one of those situations. I cannot begin to express the range of emotions and amount of stress that this can place on a leadership team. It has been suggested to me that we are a bunch of "bleeding hearts" and should have nothing to do with people like this. I have endured the reproach of those who have called me naïve to think that this man won't offend again and I have encountered those from the other end of the spectrum who were so full of forgiveness and love that they suggested throwing all caution to the wind and just trusting God.

Doing things God's way has always been the goal of the leadership team at my church. Every church has leaders that express this value but some, when put to the test, opt to approach things from less than a Godly perspective. I am incredibly blessed to have a group of leaders that believe in restoration. When I called them together to discuss the situation and how we could work with this man, not one of them felt it was right of us to tell him that he could not attend. Because none of the people involved in his case were attending our church, or lived in our community, our team felt that we were the right people to help in the restoration process.

Before making any decisions, the following actions were taken by the church leadership:

A call was placed to a lawyer to explain the legal ramifications of any actions on the church's part. Because the church was part of a larger affiliated body, several calls were made to our District Superintendent seeking counsel. Numerous calls were made to the probation officer to better understand the restrictions that the fellow was subject to under his probation order. Several calls were made to the arresting police officer who had handled the case and to the chaplain of the institution where the man had been incarcerated. This insured that the leadership team had all the facts that were necessary to make the best decisions.

In situations like this one there are several important things for a leadership team to consider. The first and probably the most important is the safety of the congregation. Congregation members and their families can never be put at risk in the process of restoration. After talking with the probation officer and sitting through the court proceedings there was a comfort level among the team that we were capable of making sure that no one in our church, especially the youth and children were at risk during church activities. Our decision to help restore this man was made easier by the fact that none of his victims attended our church or lived in the community. If they had, our course of action would probably have been dramatically different. A victim's emotional health and safety must take precedence in these situations.

The leadership team was faced with the decision of whether or not to make a public announcement regarding this man's presence in our church. Did the congregation have a right to know that a convicted child molester was attending their church? We decided not to make a public announcement. After much investigation and evaluation it was our belief that with close supervision and a cooperative attitude from him, we could ensure the safety of the congregation, better aid in his spiritual growth and not disrupt congregational unity. The key to our decision was the man's willingness to be restored, his deep remorse and his willingness to cooperate with the process. This may not be the case in many situations and should not be taken as an example to naively welcome danger in the church but it was right for us. About one-third of the people who attend our church know about the situation and their behavior towards the man can best be described as warm, kind and careful.

Another very important element in re-introducing a child molester to a church is deciding whether or not it will adversely affect the spiritual health and growth of the abused. This particular fellow was responsible for interfering with the emotional, physical and spiritual health of two young people and behaving inappropriately with three others. This could never be trivialized. I do not believe that it is healthy for the congregation of a smaller church to try to restore the abuser and heal the abused at the same time. Church life affords too many opportunities for the abuser and the abused to be put together in close proximity which can inflict further hurt on everyone involved. In such a case, the abuser should seek another body of believers to aid in the restoration process.

An unpopular piece of the puzzle that is often overlooked by the church is the spiritual health and growth of the abuser. Although this man had committed a grievous sin he was still created by God in his image and in need of ministry. Like all of us he was a beneficiary of the grace of God and, upon sincere repentance, a part of God's family. This may be very difficult for people to take and I truly understand but we are not called to minister to the easy situations but to follow the lead of Jesus and find ways to minister to the difficult ones also.

When we had done all our homework, we sat down with the man, assured him of our support and concerns and asked him to sign a covenant document. This is a covenant that clearly outlines the guidelines under which he can participate in the life of the church. It is not mean to be punitive or to exert control over him, but in his own words it is "a document that protects me and protects the church." Although our leadership team did not author this document in it's entirety, we modified it to suit our unique situation and are eternally grateful to the original authors.

(See page 278 for the *Offender's Covenant*.)

Conclusion

Our society needs a paradigm shift. We have to change our mind-set.

Never has there been a time in this world when such a tsunami of smut has flooded humanity, drenching every aspect in images designed to increase man's libido.

Never have the purveyors of pornography had such a widespread influence of the development of our boys and girls.

Never before have pedophiles had a peer group of like-minded individuals with which they can connect any hour of the day or night, empowering and seemingly legitimizing each other through their numbers.

Never have our prisons been so crowded with sex-offenders who need to be held in isolation from the general prison populace.

There is only one solution and it can happen only individually.

Each of us needs to have our minds renewed. We need a new mind-set that values things like kindness, integrity, mentoring, patience, consideration, concern for others, gratitude, generosity, forgiveness, restorative justice and wisdom.

In the process of renewal, we need to be highly conscious of those who do not espouse the same values and be well educated as to their tactics.

The pendulum of our culture has swung far enough to the dark side, where we have experienced its results in the sex abuse of our children, the shattering of marriages, the disintegration of our families, the objectifying of our women, the disappearance of our men and women of integrity and the suicides of our despondent youth.

Only with a fresh swing of the pendulum to the light will we be able to give our children back their safe streets on which to play in the warm summer evenings. Only then will we be able to predator-proof our families with confidence.

The past is irreparable—but the future is available.

It's time to create a new, different world.

(*Please feel free to duplicate.*)

Dear ______________________________

(*Name of Offender*)

On behalf of the leadership of

____

(*Name of Church*)

Location ______________________________

Phone ______________ Primary Contact ______________

I would like to welcome you to participate in the worship and congregational life of our church. We want you to know that we see you as a very important and valued part of God's family. In light of all that has taken place in your life there are some guidelines that we feel must be followed. These guidelines are not meant to be punitive but to ensure safety and peace of mind for the congregation and yourself.

- You must refrain from all contact with children and minors while attending church functions. This includes all verbal and written communication.
- You must not volunteer or agree to lead, chaperone or participate in events involving children or youth.
- You must not transport any youth or children as part of the ministry program of the church.

Page one of three.

- The Elder Board will identify at least "two covenant partners" who must accompany you if you leave the main congregation or need to go to the public washrooms.
- You are to avoid being in the building unsupervised at all times. This includes all children's ministry areas and washroom areas. When entering the church, you must use the most direct route to the sanctuary area and sit in an area that is visible to your covenant partners.
- You are to participate throughout the duration of this covenant, in regular counseling and present verification of the same to the church leadership.
- You are to abide by the terms and conditions of probation as set out by the court.
- You must meet regularly (bi-weekly) with a member of the church leadership team for spiritual counsel and encouragement.
- You are not to be in any non-lit areas of the church property.
- You are welcome and encouraged to join one of our adult small groups if minors are not present and if the facilitator is made aware of the situation.
- At least twice per year you are requested to meet with the Board of Elders to discuss your adherence to these guidelines.
- If you relocate to another congregation you must give permission for the leadership to discuss your situation with the new congregation.

We are so grateful that you have made us aware of your situation. It shows us that there is a cooperative spirit and willingness for restoration and wholeness.

Page two of three.

I accept the following people as Covenant Partners. I agree that they will be made aware of the circumstances of my situation and the contents of this covenant.

____

Covenant Partner #1

____

Covenant Partner #2

____

Covenant Partner #3

I have read and agree to abide by the conditions of this covenant.

I understand that any violation of this covenant may result in refusal of access to the church property or congregational gatherings may be restricted or prohibited.

I understand that this covenant will be reviewed every six months and will remain in effect for an indefinite period of time.

Offender's Signature	Date
Pastoral Leader's Signature	Date

Page three of three.

For further reading...

Abel, G., Becker, J., Mittleman, M., Rouleau, J., and Murphy, W. (1987). Journal of Interpersonal Violence, 2(1), March

Beauregard, M and O'Leary, D. (2007). *The Spiritual Brain*, A Neuroscientist's Case for the Existence of the Soul, HarperOne, San Francisco, CA

The Holy Bible, The New International Version, Zondervan Bible Publishers, Grand Rapids, Michigan.

Birchall, E. (1989). The Frequency of Child Abuse – What do We Really Know?, in Colton, Matthew and Vanstone, Maurice (1996). *Betrayal of Trust*; Sexual Abuse by Men Who Work With Children, , London ON: Free Association Books Ltd.

Bremner, Dr. J. Douglas (2007). The Lasting Effects of Psychological Trauma on Memory and the Hippocampus, Law and Psychiatry,

Briggs, F., & Hawkins, R.M.F. (1996). A comparison of the childhood experiences of convicted male child molesters and men who were sexually abused in childhood and claimed to be non offenders. Child Abuse and Neglect

Browne, A., & Finkelhor, D. (1986). Initial and long-term effects: A review of the research. In D. Finkelhor, A Sourcebook on Child Sexual Abuse, Beverly Hills: Sage

Bushman, B.J., Baumeister, R.F., & Stack, A.D. (1999). *Catharsis, aggression and persuasive influence: Self-fulfilling or self-defeating prophecies?* Journal of Personality and Social Psychology

Butler, Sandra (1985). *Conspiracy of Silence: The Trauma of Incest,* San Francisco, Volcano Press.

Carnes, Patrick (1994). *Out of the Shadows*; Understanding Sexual Addiction, Center City, Minnesota: Hazelden Foundation

Carter, Wm. Lee (2002). *A Teen's Guide to Overcoming Sexual Abuse;* It Happened to Me, Oakland, Ca., New Harbinger Publications, Inc.

Colton, Matthew and Vanstone, Maurice (1996). *Betrayal of Trust*; Sexual Abuse by Men Who Work With Children, , London ON: Free Association Books Ltd.
Diagnostic and Statistical Manual of Mental Disorders (DSM 111-R), The American Psychological Association, 1987

Elliott, M., Browne, K., & Kilcoyne, J. (1995). *Child Sexual Abuse Prevention: What Offenders Tell Us*, Child Abuse & Neglect

Fink, Paul (2005). *Science,* Vol. 309, August.
Finkelhor, D. (1984). *Child Sexual Abuse: New Theory and Research*, New York: Free Press.

Finkelhor, D. and associates (eds) (1986), *A Sourcebook on Child Sexual Abuse*, Newbury Park, CA.: Sage.

Finkelhor, D., Hotaling, G., Lewis, I. and Smith, C. (1990) *Sexual Abuse in a National Survey of Adult Men and Women;* Prevalence Characteristics and Risk Factors, *Child Abuse and Neglect.*

Finkelhor, D. (1994). The International epidemiology of child sexual abuse. *Child Abuse & Neglect*, 18

Finkelhor, D. and Dziuba-Leatherman, J. (1995). Victimization prevention programs: A national survey of children's exposure and reactions, Child Abuse & Neglect

Finney, Lynne D. (1992). *Reach for the Rainbow*; Advance Healing for Survivors of Sexual Abuse, New York: The Putnam Publishing Group

Forward, Susan, and Craig Buck (1979). *Betrayal of Innocence: Incest and its Devastation,* New York: Penguin Books.

Genesee Justice Family (2005). *Genesee Justice 2005*; Instruments of Law, Order and Peace, Batavia, N.Y., Genesee Justice Family Research & Development

Groth, N., Burgess, A., Birnbaum, H. and Gary, T. (1978). A study of the child molester. Myths and realities. *LAE Journal of the American Criminal Justice Association*, 41(1), Winter/Spring.

Halliday, L. (1985). Sexual Abuse: Counseling issues and concerns. Campbell River, B.C., Ptarmigan Press

Hergenhahn, B.R. (1992). *An introduction to the history of psychology*. Belmont, CA:Wadsworth Publishing Company.

Hopper, Dr. J. (2007). Child Abuse: Statistics, Research and Resources
Jacob Wetterling Foundation web site's frequently asked questions section

Knopp, Fay Honey (1982). *Remedial Intervention in Adolescent Sex Offenses*; Nine Program Descriptions, Brooklyn, N.Y.: Faculty Press, Inc.

Leaf , Dr. Caroline (2007). Who Switched Off My Brain?, Switch on Your Brain, Rivonia, South Africa

Lilienfeld, Scott O. and Lambert, Kelly (Oct. 2007). Brain Stains, Scientific American

MacAulay, The Honourable Lawrence - Solicitor General Canada (2001). *High-Risk Offenders;* A Handbook for Criminal Justice Professionals, Ottawa, The Government of Canada

Marshall, Dr. W.L. and Barrett, Sylvia (1990). *Criminal Neglect*; Why Sex Offenders Go Free, Toronto: Doubleday Canada Limited

Matthews, Dr. Frederick (1995). *Breaking Silence - Creating Hope*; Help for Adults Who Molest Children, Ottawa: National Clearinghouse on Family Violence, Health Canada

McCoy, D. (2006). *The Manipulative Man*, Adams Media, Avon, Mass

Mercy, J. A. (1999). Having New Eyes: Viewing Child Sexual Abuse as a Public Health Problem. Sexual Abuse: A Journal of Research and Treatment

Michel, Lou and Herbeck, Dan, *Confessions of a Child Porn Addict,* The Buffalo News, Oct. 21, 2007

Minnery, Tom (1986). *Pornography; A Human Tragedy*, Wheaton, Illinois, Tyndale House Publishers Inc., Dr. J. Dobson

Murr, Doris C. (2004). *Dorie's Secret*, Kitchener, Ontario, Pandora Press

Peck, M. Scott (1983). People of the Lie, New York, Touchstone - Simon & Schuster Inc.

Posten, Carol and Lison, Karen (1990). *Reclaiming our Lives*; Hope for Adult Survivors of Incest, Boston, MA: Little, Brown & Company

Pryor, Douglas W. (1996). *Unspeakable Acts*; Why men Sexually Abuse Children, New York and London: New York University Press

Public Health Agency of Canada (2007), National Clearinghouse on Family Violence.

Reavill, Gil (2005). *Smut;* A Sex Industry Insider (and Concerned father) says Enough is Enough, London, England, Penguin Books, Ltd.

Rush, F. (1980). *The best kept secret: Sexual abuse of children.* New York, McGraw-Hill Book Company

The San Francisco Chronicle (April 3, 2005)

Salter, Anna C. (1988). *Treating Child Sex Offenders and Victims*; A Practical Guide, Newbury Park, California: SAGE Publications, Inc.

Salter, Anna C. (2003). *Predators: Pedophiles, Rapists and Other Sex Offenders* , New York: Basic Books

Science Daily, July 30, 2007. News release issued by Stanford University Medical Centre

Seligman, M.E.P. (1994). What You Can Change and What You Can't. New York: Alfred A. Knopf.

Sher, Julian (2007). *One Child at a Time,* Random House Canada

Singer, P. (1991). Ethics. *The New Encyclopedia Britannica*, Volume 18, Edition 15

UN Secretary General's Study on Violence Against Children (2006) section II.B

Van Dam, Carla (2001). *Identifying Child Molesters, Preventing Child Sexual Abuse by Recognizing the Patterns of the Offenders,* New York: The Halworth Maltreatment and Trauma Press

Wholey, Sam (1992). *When the Worst That Can Happen Already Has*; Conquering Life's Most Difficult Times, New York: Hyperion

Yantzi, Mark (1998). *Sexual Offending and Restoration*, Waterloo, Ontario and Scottdale, Pa., Herald Press

To Book a Speaking Engagement

Diane Roblin-Lee
905-852-6349
diane@bydesignmedia.ca
www.bydesignmedia.ca

For further information on

Training Workshops and Speakers,
Information and Training Materials
for *Plan to Protect*,
please contact:

Winning Kids Inc.
www.winningkidsinc.ca
1-877-455-3555

www.predatorproofyourfamily.com
www.bredatorproofyourfamily.blogspot.com

www.ingramcontent.com/pod-product-compliance
Lightning Source LLC
Chambersburg PA
CBHW060253100426
42742CB00011B/1738
* 9 7 8 1 9 2 7 3 5 5 0 0 8 *